BELIEVING CHRISTIANS . . .

. . . will here learn to enjoy and recognize the daily aspects of the Spirit-filled life. They will be guided toward a new understanding of the Scriptures, and to a growing discovery of what God expects of those baptized in the Spirit.

Those long in the faith and those newly born into it can find in this book guidelines along the path God has set—and eagerly follow the way to effective prayer and a joyous new life.

NOW THAT

YOU'VE BEEN BAPTIZED

IN THE SPIRIT ...

DONALD GEE

GOSPEL PUBLISHING HOUSE
Springfield, Missouri
02–0461

NOW THAT YOU'VE BEEN BAPTIZED IN THE SPIRIT . . .

Published by Pyramid Publications for the Gospel Publishing House

This edition published September, 1972

© 1972 by the Gospel Publishing House
All Rights Reserved

Part I first published 1945 as After Pentecost
Part II first published 1930 as The Ministry Gifts of Christ
Copyright by the Gospel Publishing House

Printed in the United States of America

GOSPEL PUBLISHING HOUSE
Springfield, Missouri 65802, U.S.A.

CONTENTS

FOREWORD

The number of Christian believers who have received the baptism in the Holy Spirit is growing at a tremendous rate. Millions are now numbered in this group, and they can be found in literally every Christian organization known to man.

New Pentecostal believers need sound, scriptural teaching, be they Catholic or Protestant. Too often they receive unscriptural teaching or none at all, and many drift aimlessly like a rudderless ship on the high seas.

Here Donald Gee offers guidance about the Holy Spirit and His activities that will make profound truths clear and simple. Charismatic believers will find this book ideal for individual or group study.

The book is divided into two parts. Part I, "Toward Christian Maturity" (previously published as *After Pentecost*) and Part II, "Gifts for the Church" (previously published as *The Ministry Gifts of Christ*).

Part I is slanted toward Christian believers—ministers and laymen—who have received the baptism in the Holy Spirit. It will be welcome counsel to believers in the traditional Pentecostal churches as well as those in the many new Pentecostal or Charismatic groups now springing up across the country and around the world.

Donald Gee emphasizes the daily aspects of the Spirit-filled life. "Our calling is to live always in the present with God—to abide. The afterward of a Pentecostal blessing is walking in the Spirit."

In Part II the author takes the reader a step further into the Spirit-filled life. Here is an excellent study on what God expects of those leaders He has "set" in the Church, particularly apostles, prophets, evangelists, pastors, and teachers. He stresses that these leaders fulfill their offices not so much by natural gifts as by spiritual power.

For many years the late Donald Gee was a leading Pentecostal preacher and writer. His pulpit and writing ministries contributed much to not only his own British Assemblies of God but to the worldwide Pentecostal Movement as well. During his long and fruitful lifetime he served as pastor, editor, writer, church official, and throughout the world as a speaker, visiting at least 60 countries. And several of his books were translated into as many as nine languages.

The publisher is pleased to add *Now that You've Been Baptized in the Spirit* to the Donald Gee book series so well received by Christians in many lands.

WAYNE E. WARNER
Editor

PART I

Toward Christian Maturity

1

After Pentecost

It is necessary to remember that almost all the writings of the New Testament that follow the four Gospels were addressed to Christians *after* Pentecost. That is to say, they were written to believers who had entered into a definite experience of the Holy Spirit in life and service comparable in all essentials to that received "at the beginning" (Acts 11:15) by the original company in the famous upper room in Jerusalem. Any converts who had not so received the Spirit were regarded as lacking a vital necessity, and steps were taken immediately to remedy the defect (Acts 8:15; 18:26; 19:2). The fact that believers knew a personal participation in the Pentecostal blessing as a well-remembered focal point in their Christian life was assumed as a basis for exhortation and argument (Galatians 3:2, 5, 14; Ephesians 1:13; 4:30).

A clear grasp of the truth that the spiritual position of the believers addressed by the various writers of the New Testament was an after-Pentecost position will help to clarify certain misunderstandings regarding believers who humbly and happily believe that in these present days the Lord Jesus has baptized them also with the same blessed Spirit. In very rightly stressing the necessity for every Christian to be filled with the Spirit as at Pentecost there is a danger of making claims, and raising expectations concerning the Spirit-filled life which are far from being supported by the testimony of the

Scriptures. The actual spiritual position of those early Christians, not in rosy idealism but in sober fact, should be candidly studied and carefully understood.

To begin with, it did not make them perfect. The Epistles are full of exhortations to holiness and warnings against sin. Indeed, it might truthfully be affirmed that sanctification is the supreme theme of the apostolic letters to the churches. The glories of Christ and His so great salvation are expounded with a view to their gracious sufficiency for the Christian to live a life of victory over the temptations of the world, the flesh, and the devil. The practical sections of the Epistles are just the application of those sublime principles to the business of everyday life in the home and family, the farm and workshop, the church, and the community.

This impressive body of teaching all implies that believers who had received the Holy Spirit in His fullness still *needed* such doctrine. There was no automatic rule that once they had started well they were certain to go on well. The very reverse was true—their going on was dependent upon a constant appropriation of sanctifying grace and power through a continually renewed fullness of the Spirit, and faithful obedience to the Word.

It was the regular care of the ministers of Christ that the believers in the various local assemblies should work out their own salvation with fear and trembling because it was God who worked in them to will and to do of His good pleasure. In Christian churches that were throbbing with the supernatural manifestations of the Holy Spirit it was found that teaching and exhortation were vital ministries of supreme importance (e.g., 1 Corinthians 12:13, 14).

It should also be noted that the introduction into the realm of the divinely supernatural provided by the baptism in the Holy Spirit with signs following did not mean that the believer's whole life thereafter was to be upon such a supernatural level that he ceased to be as other men. Far from it. The story of Paul, who was preeminently blessed in his apostolic office and ministry with miraculous gifts of the Holy Spirit, abounds with most moving, human touches. He suffered hunger and thirst, nakedness and peril, fightings without and fears within, to a superlative degree. When shipwrecked he had to swim to shore with the rest; when shivering with cold his own hands helped to gather sticks for the fire; when in prison he begged Timothy to bring him his cloak. His converts were charged to work with quietness, and eat their own bread. The daily life and witness of Christians was marked, *not* by strange exemptions from the laws of nature, but by an unlikeness to the world in things of the heart. The "mighty signs and wonders by the power of the Spirit of God" of those earliest Pentecostal missionaries were balanced by pleadings for the prayers of their friends that they might be delivered from their enemies and restored to them with joy (Roman 15). "Power from on high" still left those who tasted it very natural. It never was the will of God that it should be otherwise.

Least recognized of all by many is the plain fact that after the phenomena of initial Pentecostal experiences things just had to find their holy level in a daily, and weekly, and monthly, and yearly *walking* in the Spirit. It was not all wings. They had to learn Pentecostal pedestrianism. The few early chapters of the book of Acts, with their primitive communism among the thousands of new converts from Judaism to Christianity, are glibly quoted as though they represented the normal standard of things for the Church at all times. The fact of the matter is that the times and circumstances connected with the birth of Christianity from within the womb of Judaism were exceptional and therefore transitory. That brief pregnant epoch largely ceased with the persecution that arose about Stephen and the consequent scattering. As the gospel spread throughout the Gentile world, Christianity took on a less outwardly revolutionary character, but supplied rather the intense fire of a steady inward flame. A revolution had occurred in the hearts of the Christians which worked from within.

The experience of the individual Christian will be found parallel to the history of the Church. At great crises in the spiritual life there will occur holy and proper emotional excitement. But it is obviously impossible to make life one continual crisis! Far too many Christians strive and strain to keep up the particular feelings inseparably connected with novelty long after novelty has worn off. It is as foolish as trying to put the clock back. That is not true revival at all. It is trying to remain in childhood after we have grown to manhood. We might as well seek to recapture the early morning at high noon, or act in harvest as though it were still springtime. No. The bulk of the New Testament has been written for Christians who need to brace themselves to the call of the road, be it long or short, that constitutes the remainder of their life on earth. To walk by faith, and not by sight, is their normal method. They have become, through the glory of the Pentecostal baptism, nothing less than temples of the living God. God Himself dwells in them, and walks in them. But the "rule of the road," if we may so say, for this high and holy fellowship with the Lord Almighty will be found in separation from all that is unclean; and in a watchful and daily cleansing from all filthiness of the flesh and spirit. Put in a sentence, the Christian life after Pentecost is "perfecting holiness in the fear of God" (2 Corinthians 6:16 to 7:1).

I am quite aware that a call to face such truths may be looked upon with suspicion by those ardent souls who feel so keenly the prevailing lukewarmness within the churches. They feel, and quite rightly, that we need another crisis. They deplore the fact that many appear to have lost their first love. It may give an entirely wrong first impression that we are, after all, seeking to excuse and make respectable a settling down that calls for flaming rebuke and rousing exhortation to get "back to Pentecost" and another revival. Truth, however, can never have anything but a liberating and tonic effect. And all we have said is demonstrably true from the Scriptures. To walk in the Spirit can never be to backslide. To expound a way of life wherein the sons and daughters of the Almighty can walk with Him in joy and peace throughout the whole of life's pilgrim journey involves the very opposite to "settling down" in the living death of carnality and worldliness.

A "state of revival" does not consist of multitudes of believers all remaining in the first rapture of a new personal blessing. When we say that the Church must "get back to Pentecost" and needs revival, we must remember and understand that the Church on earth is the sum total of the individuals that compose it. It is individual Christians themselves who need Pentecostal revival. What we usually mean by a "revival" in an historic sense is a time when large numbers of believers simultaneously enter into a quickened spiritual life. They have touched once again the eternal springs of life in Christ.

There are periods when multitudes are making this vital rediscovery; there are times when only a comparatively few Christians here and there are being revived. When lukewarmness is widespread, we properly pray for an equally widespread quickening of individuals. For whether many or few, the essential spiritual crisis remains a personal matter for each one A Pentecostal revival means that a great many individual believers have entered into a personal experience of the baptism in the Holy Spirit. The continuance of such a revival means that there is a steady stream of additions to the ranks of those who have received the Promise of the Father. It does not mean that those who have received shall remain in a static condition of initial ecstasy. The hour of conversion, the glory of the Baptism in the Holy Spirit, the place of definite consecration—each will bring to the soul its own corresponding emotion. Let not those in the first flush of a new adventure in God rashly criticize those who for years have been, and still are, pressing on the upward way. And let not those who commenced long ago look wistfully at the innocent enthusiasm of the neophyte as though it were something *they* should desire. To each his own joy. Ultimately our joy must come to rest simply in God Himself.

The years pass. They did for Peter and John, and all who participated in the glory of that classic upper room. They did for Paul and Apollos, and all the others who shared in the blessing of a Pentecost as at the beginning. By the time the last books of the New Testament were being written, many already had fallen asleep in Christ; those that remained were elders in the most literal sense of the word. The aged John gloried in the term. What was his personal attitude and teaching concerning the fullness of the Spirit that had come to him so long ago in Jerusalem? Simply this, that the anointing they had received of Him proved to be abiding; and that it was the calling of the anointed ones to abide in Him (1 John 2:27).

For many of us the special thrill of the earliest years of the present gracious Pentecostal Movement cannot but become a sacred memory. Let none disparage the holy sentiment it provokes. For many more who received the Holy Spirit in subsequent years their own personal Pentecost also has become enshrined in precious retrospect. Sooner or later a similar experience will overtake the last and latest believer who has received the promise of the Father. There is nothing to be disturbed about in this; nothing to regret, nothing to resist. Our only danger lies in living in the past. Our calling is to live always in the present with God—to abide. The "afterward" of a Pentecostal blessing is walking in the Spirit. It is not the receding glow from a past hour of emotional glory; it is a path "that shineth more and more unto the perfect day."

2

Temptations of the Spirit-filled Believer

One of the most striking episodes in the life of our Lord was His period of special temptation in the wilderness. The deeply significant feature of the threefold trial that He underwent there lies in the fact that it all happened *after* He had been filled with the Holy Spirit at Jordan.

Luke's references to the Holy Spirit in connection with the life of Christ are very instructive. First of all He was born of the virgin Mary through a direct operation of the Holy Spirit (Luke 1:35). Second, He received an entirely new experience of the Holy Spirit when He was about thirty years of age as an enduement of power for His public ministry (3:21, 22); third, He was definitely led by that same Spirit, with which He was now "full," into the wilderness to be tempted by the devil (4:1, 2); and finally He returned in the power of the Spirit out of the period of testing and proceeded with His brief but mightily anointed period of public ministry (4:14-18).

It is easy to see how exactly, in all its broad features, the disciple of Christ follows His Master in these various steps of experience. The Christian is first of all born of the Spirit; later, exactly like his Master, he receives the baptism in the Spirit as a separate experience enduing him with power for service. Then?

Failure to understand the significance for ourselves of the period of testing in the wilderness has resulted in much disappointment. It is seldom realized that the first forty days after receiving the Baptism in the Spirit are often among the most critical in the Christian life. Zealous and devoted Pentecostal workers will often spend days and nights helping hungry hearts *into* the blessing of the Spirit-filled life, and then they strangely leave them at the threshold with a mistaken impression that all will now be perfectly straightforward. Alas that many lives that might have been useful for God are therefore still floundering in that "wilderness!"

Lest the subject be misunderstood it ought to be very clearly shown that the equivalent of the "wilderness" experience in our own lives is not necessarily a time of spiritual declension or dryness through backsliding, but rather the opposite. It is a time of personal testing, *under power*, to prove the capability of the human vessel to be trusted with a mighty anointing for service. When that great liner the *Queen Mary* left the shipyards, she was put through some service test *under power* before she was finally considered approved for her record-breaking Atlantic crossings. Such trials were impossible while still quietly resting in the dock; so there are spiritual temptations which are impossible to the believer until *after* he has been filled with the Spirit.

The Pentecostal experience brings the Christian into

an entirely new spiritual realm, involving not only new power, new joy, and new fellowship, but also new temptations.

The three temptations that came to the Spirit-filled Christ were typical and comprehensive. It has been pointed out that they appealed to the lust of the flesh, the lust of the eyes, and the pride of life. We might also see how they included the world, the flesh, and the devil. Turning to them in particular, we note that they consisted of testings that we too face.

Turning Stones Into Bread.

This was the temptation to use the newly given power for selfish purposes: to feed Himself, rather than the hungry multitudes who would soon be waiting for a heavenly meal.

The same test comes to all who are newly filled with the Spirit; it is the temptation to spiritual and "Pentecostal" selfishness, to break the supreme law of love (1 Corinthians 13) which always places others first and self last.

For some it mainly consists of a resolve thoroughly to enjoy their own particular manifestations of the Spirit on any and every occasion, without any thought or care for the profit, convenience, or feelings of others. This leads to many of the common extravagances and abuses of tongue and other gifts of the Holy Spirit.

With others it is a deliberate use of the manifestations of the Spirit to gain prominence for themselves in almost every meeting, to force themselves to the front, and make people take notice of them. Often there lurks in the background a love of office and a subtle desire for the praise of men. Such are noticeably quick to take offence if their presumed exercise of spiritual gifts is not immediately received with open arms.

Only in a very few cases is there the opportunity to turn the gifts of the Spirit into a means of personal gain. It is fortunate this is so, for hardly anything seems more despicable than using these precious treasures bought for the believer by the blood of God's Son as a means of financial gain.

The victory over this temptation in every case is denial of self and the flesh, and a life of walking in the Spirit.

Worshiping Satan.

The daring effrontery of this temptation as presented to our Lord seems almost unbelievable. Its significance is better understood if we remember that our Redeemer came to win back a lost world, and that this was an offer to give Him the apparent achievement of His purpose *without the cross.*

For ourselves the same temptation comes when we also are tempted to compromise with the spirit of this world and to reject the way of our own personal cross. Many worship the "god of this world" in spirit, though they would revolt at any suggestion of direct Satan worship as a cult.

The temptation to play with worldliness is not so likely to come in the first rush of a new Pentecostal blessing while the novelty is still strong upon us and the "expulsive power of a new affection" is surging within the soul. The danger occurs when the first flush has subsided; and it becomes acute if lack of attention to continual fellowship with Christ has caused love to become a little lukewarm.

Worldliness must be watched like a snake. We are always surrounded with so many things in the world which are not sinful in themselves, but which become so through abuse. This is true of food, drink, clothing, music, physical exercises, automobiles, and a host of other good things. Take for instance radio and television. These have proved a great power in the gospel. Yet some preachers dismiss their Sunday evening altar services earlier than the working of the Spirit justifies, simply because they want to hurry home to watch a certain program. No wonder they have lost the secret of their spiritual power. And the same type of thing on other lines has ruined many another once powerful testimony.

Our Lord's remedy was a positive worship of the Lord our God. For the life of victory over the world we must maintain deep worship of the Father in spirit and in truth, and this involves not only outward forms of worship but full obedience and consecration of all we have, all we are, and all we hope to be. True worship always has its sacrifices; and the way of sacrifice is the only way to keep the power of the Spirit fresh in the life.

The Pinnacle of the Temple.

The suggestion to Christ that He should throw Himself down from the pinnacle of the temple was a temptation to become a fanatic. It was the most subtle of all because it came in a religious garb, and the tempter actually quoted Scripture. Quite possibly it might have involved suicide. Our Lord knew at once that it would be sheer presumption to act on the devil's apparently scriptural suggestion; for it meant straining a promise out of all legitimate application, and virtually amounted to a misquotation of Scripture.

This type of temptation has proved deadly to multitudes as far as a profitable Pentecostal testimony and ministry has been concerned. And it is the especial temptation of those who are deeply consecrated and have successfully overcome the other two types of temptation. On high pinnacles of spiritual experience we all need to exercise great care. Lack of balance in such a position can prove deadly, and the devil knows it.

Our Lord's method of countering this temptation is full of practical significance. He met the tempter's distorted application of a verse out of the Bible by saying: "It is written *again*" (Matthew 4:7). His wide knowledge of *all* the Scriptures (actually the quotation He used was taken from Deuteronomy!) defeated the subtility of the devil. We are on a dangerous ground when we adopt some extreme and fantastic notion just because we seem to see ground for it in one or two isolated texts out of the Bible. We are called to stand on a *Book*, not on a few texts.

Those who long for a life in the peace and power of the continued fullness of the Spirit must seek a deep knowledge of the Word of God in all its parts. It is a deep, reverent heart knowledge of the great principles of the Bible that gives the Christian sound judgment and a steady poise when many others are being carried off their feet by strange doctrines and irresponsible impulses.

The perfect victory of our glorious Leader and then His subsequent return to Galilee in the *power* of this Spirit fills us with hope for our own victory also. He was tempted in all points, and not least in His Spirit-filled experience, exactly as we are; and for that very reason He is able to help them that are tempted. He ever lives for that purpose.

With our eyes upon Christ, and with His Word and His Spirit enthroned in our hearts, we can overcome even as He overcame. Our great weakness in the Pentecostal experiences at which we have been looking in this study is that we have not been watchful enough. The purpose of the Word is that it be a lamp unto our feet and a light unto our path. Thank God for the ever-increasing number who, in the light of that beacon of truth, are now coming up out of the wilderness of testing, leaning on the Beloved, vessels unto honor, sanctified, and suitable for the Master's use. Earth's crowded highways and byways still await those who in some humbler measure can echo the words of our Lord, "The Spirit of the Lord God is upon me, because He hath anointed me to preach the gospel to the poor; to heal the brokenhearted."

3

Disappointing Baptisms

This chapter deals with a difficult subject; perhaps I should say a somewhat delicate subject. It is what I call "disappointing Baptisms."

I can speak about this with courage because we know there are Baptisms that are not disappointing. Thank God, there is a glorious baptism in the Holy Spirit that never disappoints Him in us and never disappoints us, but means a continual unfolding, a richer and greater experience of the Spirit's power and the Spirit's grace. But in a fairly long experience that has been world wide I have come to the place where I feel I should consider this subject.

There are people who apparently have had the baptism in the Holy Spirit, but for some reason they have not made good, and the results are not what they ought to have been. The Word says in Acts 1:8, "Ye shall receive power after that the Holy Ghost is come upon you." We have met people who have had the Holy Spirit but have not had power. Now no advantage is ever gained by refusing to face difficulties. I love to face difficulties; that is the way we learn. If we have a problem let us get hold of it and put it under the searchlight of God's Word and the searchlight of prayer until God has given us the solution of it. That is how we learn in the progress of aviation. We have had terrible disasters but do we say we will not fly any more? We get to work at once to discover why this disaster occurred. What was the weakness that caused the crash? And when we have found the cause of the trouble, what do we do? We proceed at once to rectify the error and make the weak places strong. Consequently, aviation becomes more and more trustworthy.

As in the natural, so in the spiritual. When we see a weakness, a failure, or a crash, let us not refuse to think about it, but bring it out in the light of God's holy truth and find out what the Lord has to teach us. Now when I am speaking of people who have been baptized in the Holy Spirit I am taking the scriptural position of the sign of tongues accompanying the Baptism. When people receive this experience there ought to be power in their lives, and yet we meet God's children where this is not the case. Let us find the difficulty.

I want to group what I call disappointing Baptisms under three headings. The first group are the people who have experienced no difference in their lives after the Pentecostal baptism. I thank God for the multitude whose lives are absolutely changed by the Baptism in the Holy Spirit. I am one of them. But there are people who say they have the Baptism and speak with tongues and yet after a few years or weeks have gone by they do not seem to be any different in their lives. Something is wrong somewhere, I am sure. A real Baptism will make a tremendous difference.

The second group are people who, when they receive the baptism in the Holy Spirit, received some of the gifts of the Spirit, but they do not have any fruit of the Spirit. They seem to be able to speak in tongues but do not have love. They have outward manifestations of the Spirit but we are sorry to say their lives and testimonies are very far from what they ought to be; there is something wrong with a baptism in the Holy Spirit that only gives people gifts and doesn't make them more holy. It is a disappointing baptism—if not to them, it is to others.

And then the last group are those who have gifts and also fruit and yet who do not have any real power. They can speak with tongues and their lives are blameless, but you could not really say that they have power in their lives. They are not powerful Christians and yet the Book says, "Ye shall have power after that the Holy Ghost is come upon you."

First of all let us consider this group where people have had the experience of the baptism in the Holy Spirit and yet we do not seem to see any difference in their lives, and they themselves confess they do not feel any different. My suggestion is this: If God has genuinely filled you with the Holy Spirit and you allow doubt and fear and unbelief to come in, they will paralyze the effect of the baptism in the Spirit in your life and testimony. If you doubt what God has done for you, the very thing He has done ceases to be operative in your life. If you let fear come in you become paralyzed.

Several years ago in London, there was a brother in our assembly, a fine young fellow, an earnest, clean, upright Christian. He came to the altar to pray but nothing ever seemed to happen. We prayed for him, we laid hands on him, and did all we could, but it seemed we might as well pray with a brick for all that resulted. We became puzzled and perplexed. Why was it? At last one day I talked with him alone: "Look here, brother, we have to get down to the root of this. Tell me, have you ever had an experience in the past when God has blessed you with a visitation of His Spirit's power?" "Yes," he said, "about seven or eight months ago I had a wonderful blessing. One night the Spirit of God came upon me in power. I was so lost in God I didn't know what happened. They tell me that I spoke in tongues. That is what they tell me, but you know I do not believe it." "Oh!" I said, "you need say no more. That is the explanation. You do not believe it." God had baptized that man in the Holy Spirit, and after he had that blessed experience he said he did not believe it. Immediately he became exactly in the same position as one who never had had the Baptism at all; the blessing God had given was paralyzed; the power was frozen. I said, "What you need to do is to thank the Lord for what He has done, and it would not be out of place for you to ask Him to forgive you." The next meeting he asked the Lord to forgive his months of unbelief, and in a minute there was a divine explosion of power. What a time we had! The living water began to flow in rivers. You might have a disappointing Baptism because you have gone back on what God has done for you, because you have denied the experience. The Lord help us to thank Him with believing hearts for what He has done for our souls.

There is another thing I want to say, and I say it regretfully. I believe that some Baptisms are disappointing because some people have been urged to speak in what seemed to be tongues, and I doubt if they have really had the Baptism at all. I say very frankly that one of the curses that has marred this Pentecostal Movement has been that of forcing people to speak in tongues when the Holy Spirit has not been acting. Speaking in tongues does not bring the Spirit; it is the Spirit that brings the tongues. When people are filled with the Holy Spirit they will speak without someone trying to force them to do it. They will be so full that they cannot contain it. God cleanse this lovely Movement from this vile travesty of the real. The methods of some of our altar workers bring reproach upon the work. I'd rather wait ten years and have something from God than to have a manifestation of the flesh without any power. I am afraid that people who were forced to speak in tongues have never had the Baptism. I do not wonder that their lives have not been changed. Beware of forcing people into the experience. I fear some are tempted to push people into the Baptism in order to pile up statistics of people receiving the experience under their ministry. The net results for eternity of ten Holy Spirit baptisms will be better than a thousand of the other sort, and the judgment seat at which we will be brought to give an account of our works will reveal the motives. Thank God for those who are always working in the shadow of that great day where we shall give an account of our stewardship.

The real Baptism is a bubbling forth of the Spirit within; you are so bursting with joy your ordinary language cannot express the feeling within. I used all the English I could muster, the full extent of my vocabulary, and I had more praise in my heart and more worship for Jesus than I could utter. I got against a brick wall, as it were, and I hadn't any words to speak to Him as I had used up all mine; so He gave me His and I spoke in tongues as the Spirit gave me utterance. I say to the critics of this Movement, there is a real, and when we have purged out the rubbish the real will shine forth in power.

Now I want to speak of those who make a big outward show of the gifts of the Spirit but seem to have very little of the fruit, very little holiness; their lives are not showing the grace of our Lord Jesus Christ. These are the people who do more harm to the Pentecostal testimony than all the writers and preachers who have written and spoken against it put together. Our greatest enemies are not those outside the Movement. You might as well try to stop Niagara as to try to stop this Movement. I laugh when I read their pamphlets and hear their sermons against Pentecost. In Great Britain we have had everybody of the Christian church solidly against Pentecost. From the Church of England down to the Salvation Army, all have fought our testimony. The cream of the Bible teachers in the world have sharpened their pens to write against this Movement. Today the Pentecostal work in England is rolling on in greater magnitude than ever, and the largest halls in Great Britain are necessary to hold the crowds. I used to worry when somebody brought out a new booklet. I'd have a bad night, could scarcely sleep, but the attacks from without have not hurt us. Sad to say, the Movement has been weakened, held back and injured by the enemies inside, and the enemies on the inside are those who speak "with tongues of men and angels and have not love." May God give us to see that there is something radically wrong with the experience that gives you gifts and doesn't give you holiness.

He is the Spirit of truth and when we love the truth it will always help us. So looking again for help, I think one of the reasons—here perhaps I will utter a word of defense for the Movement—one of the reasons is that we have looked in the wrong place for the fruit of the Spirit. We have confused the gifts of the Spirit and the fruit of the Spirit, and we have thought that the baptism in the Spirit was to produce fruit, which, of course, is a mistake. Fruit comes from Christ in the heart. The result of the baptism in the Holy Spirit is supernatural gifts. Now we receive the Spirit of Christ in our hearts in regeneration and in that sense we receive the Holy Spirit as the Spirit of Christ. That is different from receiving Him in His own wonderful, distinctive personality. The Holy Spirit is revealed as the Spirit of the Father, He is revealed as the Spirit of the Son, and He also has a separate, distinct personality. Let me illustrate. Sometime ago I had a letter from a certain brother who is a secretary of a church in England, asking me to come and have some meetings in that church. He wrote me an official letter, on the official stationery of the church and signed at the end with his own name and underneath, "Church Secretary." It was a very business-like, official letter. But it so happened that this particular brother was also a personal friend of mine and took advantage of sending an official letter as the secretary to put in a personal word, so on a slip of ordinary paper he scribbled a personal note in his own familiar scrawl: "Dear Donald: I am enclosing an official note from the church. I do hope you will come and that you can come and stay at our house. Yours ever, Stanley." Both letters were from the same man but in one he wrote as the secretary of the church and in the other as a personal friend. This is the best illustration I can give of the two aspects of the Holy Spirit. It is not two Spirits, it is One. In one He comes as the Spirit of Christ because Christ in His own Person is seated at the Father's right hand. Yet I can say with Paul, "Christ liveth in me." How can Christ live in me except by the Spirit? Christ is in heaven but I am glad that by His Spirit He is dwelling in my heart.

Now what I am really wanting to give you is that it is from the Spirit of Christ in our hearts that the fruit of the Spirit comes. What did Jesus teach us in the 15th chapter of John? He said, "He that abideth in me, and I in Him, the same bringeth forth much fruit." In Philippians it speaks of "being filled with the fruits of righteousness which are by Jesus Christ," and when Christ is in your heart you will have love, joy, peace, long-suffering, and all the fruit of the Spirit.

Now it is possible to have all this; it is possible to walk with Christ and have all this and yet not have the fullness of the Pentecostal baptism. That is why people say, "Look at all those beautiful Christians with their holy lives. They never have had this Baptism." Yes, they are beautiful and we thank God for their lives. What is the explanation? They have Christ in their hearts, they are walking and living with Him. Thank God the character of Jesus Christ is revealed in our lives.

The Pentecostal baptism brings us in touch with the supernatural power of God. We need, not only the fruit of the Spirit but we need the gifts. We need, not only to be built up in character but we need the dynamic power of God. But the trouble is some people who have the baptism in the Holy Spirit and have had a touch of the supernatural have not walked with Jesus and lived close to Him. They haven't kept that life of private communion with God; they haven't walked in the light of His Word or obeyed it, and they wonder why their lives are hollow. If we have the Spirit of Jesus we need to walk close to Him, so that along with the gift we have the fruit. Do not think that speaking in tongues will ever take the place of walking with God. The source of holiness is Christ, and the source of fruit is Christ enthroned in the heart and life. That is why some people have disappointing baptisms; they have broken communion with the Lord; they have not walked in the Spirit. God help us to abide in Christ and have the fruit of holiness in our lives.

Now I have to say something which I am afraid is

contrary to the belief of many, that speaking in tongues is nowhere given in the Scriptures as a sign of spiritual health. People say, "Oh, we know we are going on with God because we are speaking in tongues every day!" Can you show me the Bible passage, my friend? As the initial sign of the baptism in the Holy Spirit to prove that He has come and filled the temple, I thank God that it is invaluable, but it is no sign that one is walking with God.

The same is true with regard to people's attitude in a meeting. Some think that as long as they can preach they are right spiritually; as long as they can lead in prayer or testify, they think they are in health spiritually; they say, "Oh, I am all right! Look how I can take part in a meeting!" The test of your spiritual life is not what you are in a meeting. It is what you are when you are alone with God. I say it without fear of contradiction. A man may make a big show and deceive the people into thinking that he walks with God, but the test of his soul is how does he look when alone with God. Some of us love to pray in public, but do we love secret prayer? Some of us love to feel the glory and enthusiasm of a crowd, especially in a live, revival meeting, but we shrink from the Garden of Gethsemane. When in a great spiritual meeting you say, "I feel grand!" but brother, the test of your spiritual life is whether you feel grand when alone with God; when the hours spent in His presence are like heaven on earth.

I suppose the most striking illustration of this is King Saul. You will remember that when he disobeyed God, the Spirit of the Lord departed from him, and yet after that there came a time when he was among the prophets, that the Spirit of the Lord came upon him and he prophesied. That was when he was backslidden and his heart was a raging inferno, and he was determined to murder David. You ask, "How did it happen that he prophesied when his heart was in that condition?" It may not fit in with your theory, but it happened. It is in the Book. What is the explanation? You will find that Saul comes into an atmosphere that is charged with the Spirit's power. He comes among Samuel and the prophets. They are under God's anointing and prophesy as the Spirit is upon them. As I have said the atmosphere is charged with the presence of the Lord, and in the heavenly atmosphere Saul comes under the influence and the Spirit moves him also for a little time. It is just a revival of the old manifestation he used to have in the days when he walked with God.

I have seen it happen again and again; people who were backslidden, who had lost the anointing, have come into conventions and revivals and when they got into a spiritual atmosphere they again had the touch of the Spirit upon them; but the whole thing is the result of the atmosphere. The test of a man's soul is when he is alone with God. When King Saul was alone he was so distracted, so beside himself, they used to get a musician to soothe him. Brother, sister, how is it with your soul when you are alone with Jesus? I do not ask how it is when you are in a meeting. I believe many of us have the choicest, happiest moment in our lives when we are shut in with God. Out of that fellowship comes real holiness and fruit of the Spirit. I say, too, that success in the ministry is no measure of your own spiritual life. May the Lord help us as ministers of the gospel to realize that while we are working in His vineyard we have one of our own to cultivate, and while we are sowing and planting in the garden of the Lord, there is a little plot in our hearts we must not neglect. Remember the words of the great preacher, Paul, "I keep under my body, and bring it into subjection: lest that by any means, when I have preached to others, I myself should be a castaway."

The last group about which I wish to talk are those who have had the experience of the baptism in the Holy Spirit yet who do not seem, somehow, to have power nor any real fruitfulness; they don't seem to have ever had the outflow of the rivers of living water of which the Scriptures speak. There is every reason to believe their experience is genuine; they have had gifts of the Spirit, their lives are beautiful, but there is that lack of power and fruitfulness. Some readers, no doubt, are saying in their hearts, "Brother Gee, will you speak a word that will help me?"

Believers in this group must learn an important lesson. We need to wait upon God even after He has given gifts of the Spirit. They are not automatic. We read in Romans 12:6-8, "Having then gifts differing according to the grace that is given to us, whether prophecy, let us prophesy according to the proportion of faith; or ministry, let us wait on our ministering; or he that teacheth, on teaching; or he that exhorteth, on exhortation." We have to wait on our gifts so that they can produce the real fruit God intends them to produce. So many people have a mistaken idea that the baptism in the Holy Spirit does away with all need of hard work. I love to impress this upon our students at our Bible schools; the baptism in the Holy Spirit is not a labor-saving device. You say, "I suppose I won't need to study; I won't need to think; I won't need to pray." That is the very reason so many people who have had the baptism in the Spirit have no ministry. They have had gifts but have never been diligent. Oh, the childish babbling in tongues that we hear in some places! There is nothing convincing or beautiful or powerful about it. I am not talking of those who have recently received the experience, but of those who have had it for years. It is just the same with interpretation and prophesying. Some is so infantile, fragmentary.

"Forasmuch as you are zealous of spiritual gifts, seek

that ye may excel." Some of the sayings that are supposed to come from the gift of prophecy are so childish it is wrong to make the Holy Spirit responsible for it. Real prophecy is magnificent. It has revelation in it. It has something which makes our hearts burn. It is the same with the word of wisdom and the word of knowledge. If God has given you these gifts, you have to *wait* on Him that they may be developed. You may have possibilities as a teacher and a preacher that are supernatural because of the baptism in the Holy Spirit, but even a gift from God you have to be at your best with it. *"He that exhorteth,"* Paul says, let him wait, develop his exhortation by every means in his power.

The parable our Lord gave to teach us this truth is the parable of the talents. Here were the servants, and the Lord gave them gifts; they were not the servants' property but given to them with which to trade. Two of them went to business with them, but one man dug a hole in the ground and buried it. He didn't lose his gift; it wasn't taken away from him until the day of reckoning. When that day came he dug it out and said, "Here you are, Lord. Here is your pound." He didn't lose anything, but he didn't gain anything either. May the Lord help us to see that we have to be diligent with our gifts. Perhaps that is why you haven't had the results for which you have longed. You thought the gift would work itself. It will not. Our spiritual gifts have to be traded with; that is the lesson in the parable. They have to be diligently developed that we may get the best returns for God and man. And perhaps you haven't prayed enough that God will give you further gifts. The Bible says, "Covet earnestly the best gifts." Be diligent. Pray for them. Perhaps the gift you have will not give you very much fruit, but ask God to give you one that will. Oh, that we might long to be useful in these days when the field is white unto harvest! The Lord help us to seek His face to show us how to use His sickle that is sharp and clean.

I am not talking now about great outward results that men speak about. I am talking about that sweet sense of the things that God is doing. I am not speaking of evangelistic work. God has other offices in the church that are of equal importance.

Timothy received a gift from God. It came with prophecy. He had a real gift and yet Paul said to Timothy, "Stir up the gift," or as the Greek has it, "rekindle the gift." We hear people pray, "O Lord, stir up my gift," but the Book tells you to stir it up yourself. "Neglect not the gift that is in thee." How can you do it? Suppose you have a fire almost on the point of going out, and you wanted to rekindle it. What should you do? I'd get down on my knees and start building it. If you want to rekindle go to your knees and breathe that heavenly breath, the breath of prayer.

Another thing to do if a fire is going out, is to get some more wood. God still has lots of wood for the heavenly fire if you will go and gather it. There is a lot of fuel in His Book. "While I was musing the fire burned." Don't expect the anointing of the Spirit to make up for your laziness. Get fresh things from God; more wood for the fire. Don't preach the old sermons over and over. I heard a man preach sometime ago, and to be honest I believe it was the sixth time I had heard that sermon.

There is another sort of wood which has a wonderful rekindling effect when you get together, "Forsake not the assembling of yourselves together." Bless God for the times when we kindle the flame in each other's hearts. Ah, yes, we have a responsibility. Do not say, "The Spirit did not move me." Perhaps He was willing for you to move yourself. We are co-workers with God. I have to work with the Spirit. I cannot drag the Spirit along behind me, but I work hand in hand with God. Oh, this divine cooperation is wonderful! As I, like Elijah of old, set my sacrifice in order, and put my bullock upon it and the wood, He sends the fire.

Now I want to close this chapter with the deepest thought of all, and God knows I am speaking to myself. I believe the deepest reason why so many who have had the baptism in the Spirit and the gifts of the Spirit and yet have not somehow made good and had real life and power and ministry, is this: They haven't welcomed the cross into their lives. I am not talking about blessing in His cross for salvation. I am speaking now of taking up one's cross and following Him. Many who have had a glorious Baptism have absolutely lost out because they haven't taken up their cross and followed it after Pentecost. The outflow of the Spirit depends upon death to self. You may say, "Oh, I want an easy time; I want lots of friends, popularity, money, and plenty of leisure." If you think you can be popular, have the power of the Spirit in your life and be without the cross, you are making a tremendous mistake. The people who have a real fragrant ministry for God and souls do not have their cross on display, but it is in their lives; they know what it is to die daily. Like Paul of old they say, "Death worketh in me," and everywhere they go, because they are dying to themselves, they put life in others.

Dear friend, have I put my finger on the spot? Is it so with you that you haven't really welcomed dying to yourself? that you haven't welcomed the part of suffering and self-denial, and because you have not welcomed it, there is not the desired result coming from your Baptism? Thank God there is a cross waiting for you that you can take up! And may you say, "By the help of God I will take up my cross and follow the Lamb whither soever He goeth." And as you bear your cross you will find a power in your life; from your innermost being will flow rivers of living water upon thirsty souls. Never think that the fullness of the Spirit will ever flow out of a man who seeks a life of ease. He may have an outward appearance of being successful, but there is a canker at the heart and in a short time, only a few years perhaps, the whole thing will end in smoke. There is only one place from which life comes—out of death. Life comes from the cross. That is why Jesus said so pointedly, "If any man will come after Me, let him deny himself and take up his cross and follow Me. So shall he be My disciple."

The Lord grant that none of us may have disappointing Baptisms. May He give us the fullness of the Spirit that will shine more and more unto the perfect day, so that when we see Him we can render an account of our stewardship with joy, and He will say, "Well done, thou good and faithful servant."

4

Divine and the Human Side of Sanctification

Sanctification is one of the words which we use most frequently and understand least of all. What is sanctification? There are most hazy and conflicting ideas among God's people as to its meaning, and yet there is a great hunger today for real sanctification, which is one of our deepest necessities. I do not believe any words could express too strongly the urgent need of a deeper sanctification among the ranks of those baptized in the

Holy Spirit, for our greatest enemies today are not from the outside but from within. I am concerned that this movement of God be kept pure.

First of all, what is sanctification? No doubt you know that the literal and primary meaning is *something set apart*. To sanctify anything or anybody is to set that thing or person apart; so sanctification is the act of setting apart. Dr. Moffatt translates it *consecration*.

The best illustration comes to me from my boyhood days in the old home in London where mother had a special tea service. Don't I remember that special tea service! It was of good china and delicately hand-painted with lovely ribbons and flowers and if there was anything in our home which was "sanctified" it was that tea set; it was set apart. Ordinarily it was kept most carefully shut up in the cupboard, and only on special occasions such as Christmas day and on birthdays was it brought out. It was sanctified. You may smile at such an illustration, but that tea service was surely set apart.

But let me give you an illustration from the Word of God. I suppose the finest illustration of what it is to be sanctified will be found in connection with the holy vessels which were used in the service of the temple; they could not be used for ordinary purposes or by man for man. They were sanctified vessels, set apart for one thing only and that was the service of the worship of Jehovah. You remember that Belshazzar, the king, filled up his cup of iniquity and settled his doom on the night when in a drunken feast he said, "Bring out the vessels which my father took from Jerusalem." They brought them out, and it says that he and his wives, his nobles and princes, drank wine out of the sanctified vessels, and in that hour the handwriting appeared on the wall, and that same night Belshazzar the king was slain. He had touched the sacred and sanctified vessels. Oh, sanctification is a solemn thing!

Now there is a secondary thought in the word sanctification, and that is *cleansing*. When we talk about being sanctified, we usually mean being cleansed. That is true, but that is the secondary thought and not the primary. If a thing is set apart for Jehovah's use, then it follows as certain as night follows day, that it must be clean, because He is holy. He says, "Be ye holy, for I am holy."

Let me give you another illustration. You know we in Britain are old-fashioned enough to have a king and queen and for them we keep a special royal train. I have seen it many times bringing them to Edinburgh, and in a very special sense that royal train is a sanctified train; the rest of us never use it. When it is not being used by the king and queen it is carefully kept in the sheds. Now you will see at once that because it is a royal train it must be kept scrupulously clean, for who would think of bringing it out and having the king and queen find that inside it was all smothered with dirt and cobwebs? The fact that it is set apart for royalty necessitates that it be kept clean. I believe you see the force of the meaning now—set apart for God, and because set apart for God, holy, clean, and pure.

If we wanted final proof that the primary meaning is not cleansing, but rather consecration, we have it in the use of the word in the record of Jesus where it says, "*The Father sanctifies His Son.*" God did not clean up His Son. And then the Lord Jesus Himself said, "For their sakes I sanctify myself." But the Lord Jesus did not cleanse Himself for our sakes. I thank God that He had nothing from which to cleanse Himself. One of our supreme beliefs is that our blessed Redeemer was eternally and essentially sinless and spotless; the Lamb slain for redemption was a spotless Lamb, and yet Jesus said, "I sanctify myself." It simply means that He consecrated Himself; He set Himself apart.

Now having a grip on the real meaning, I want you to consider with me the two aspects of sanctification. If we can get our balance we shall get the truth, but the great trouble today on every hand is the lack of balance. The great passion of my heart is to keep in the center of the road because on either side is a ditch and once you get in, it is a job to get out.

First, I want you to look with me at the divine side and then at the human side, and in the balancing of the two we have the great secret of sanctification. I shall begin at the very top—with Jesus Christ. Let us look at the divine side as revealed in the Son of God as given in John 10:36, "Say ye of him whom the Father hath sanctified, and sent into the world . . ." Here is our first great revelation of divine sanctification—the Father taking His Son, sanctifying Him and sending Him forth. Not purifying Him, for there was nothing impure in Him but *consecrating* Him and sending Him forth into the world. Immediately we are lifted into that glorious place that is beyond human conception, that wonderful time away in the counsels of eternity when God was longing to send a redeemer to redeem us from our sin, and sweeping His eye—as we try to imagine with holy reverence—over the assembled armies of heaven, He gazed at the archangel and this angel, and He says, "Whom shall I send?" And as He looked at that holy, glittering company He found there was none good enough to pay the price of sin, only One who was able to unlock the gates of heaven to let us in. Looking around that holy company He knew that His only Son was the One to send; so God separated, set apart, His Son; God sanctified Him and sent Him into the world. "For God so loved the world that He gave His only begotten Son." He sanctified the dearest treasure of His heart.

Next, I want you to consider with me how God has sanctified to Himself chosen vessels, and I would take you first of all to the Old Testament. Turn to Jeremiah 1:5, where you will see again the primary meaning of sanctification. God says to Jeremiah, "Before thou wast born I sanctified thee." The Lord didn't have to purify Jeremiah, for he had done nothing wrong; he didn't have to be cleansed, for he had not had time to get soiled.

Then let me take you to a New Testament case that is indeed famous. Turn to the Epistle to the Galatians 1:15, "But when it pleased God, who separated me from my mother's womb." Here the apostle Paul declares that he was sanctified from his very birth: indeed, during all those years when Paul was so rebellious, all those years when he was persecuting the church of Christ, in the divine primary sense of the word he was sanctified even then, for God had set him apart "from his mother's womb." All that time God had a hook in Paul; on that day when he watched the stones crushing the life out of Stephen, God had His hook in him, and on that never-to-be-forgotten day near the gate of Damascus, God landed His fish. I don't wonder God said to him, "Paul, it is hard for thee to kick." If you are kicking against the same mighty Lord, take my advice and give up today. If you do not, you are just laying up trouble for yourself.

So you see in the illustrations from both the Old and New Testaments what is the primary thought of sanctification; God sanctifying even from the very day of birth—"I have chosen thee. I have ordained thee. Thou art mine." And the strong confidence of my soul in these days when men's hearts are failing them for fear is that if God needs a man, He will get the right one. I believe that in every age, when God has wanted a man, He has had one, and He will not lack for the right man today. Thank God for the glorious comfort of this vision of a divine setting apart!

And now we must needs turn to ourselves. Are you ready for yourself? Turn to 1 Corinthians 1:2, "Unto the church of God which is at Corinth, *to them that are sanctified in Christ Jesus,* called to be saints." And then in the sixth chapter we read, "But *ye are washed,* but *ye are sanctified,* but *ye are justified.*" Now a moment's reading of the First Epistle to the Corinthians will prove instantly that those people were not without spot or blemish, not by a long way, and yet the apostle said, *"Ye are sanctified."* A finished work! Oh, can it be that they were sanctified? Yes, they were, but oh, the spots and blemishes and wrinkles and such things as I would hardly like to name marred the testimony of the saints of Corinth, and yet the one who knew them through and through wrote to them and said, *"Ye are sanctified."* What does it mean?

I think of all the definitions of sanctification I have found, the best is that given by Dr. Massey: "Separated in principle from sin to God through union with Christ." I do pray that God may help us to see more clearly than ever before the true separation of the Christian from the world. As soon as you are born again you are separated from those who are not born again; as a child of the light you are separated from the children of darkness; as soon as you are in the church you are separated from those who are outside the real church. We all know that the church simply means those who are called out. "Come out from among them and be separate," sanctified in Christ Jesus unto Christ Jesus; set apart. I am so happy that Christ has separated me. As truly as the children of Israel, who had the blood sprinkled on the door posts, were separated; as truly as the light shone in the houses of the children of Israel when inky blackness was on all the land, so I am separated from the world. *If you don't want to be separated from the world in its sinful pleasure, you have no right to expect to be separated from the world's woe.* Many want to be separated from the world when it plunges into tribulation, but they want a part in its sinful pleasures, and that is not possible.

I believe the best illustration of the divine side of sanctification is given us in the picture of one going down into the market place. I have seen those Eastern market places with all their junk and rubbish. The picture is of one who has gone there and seen some old vessel perhaps of brass or silver; it is dirty and covered with slime and rust and thrown away, but the connoisseur says, "There is intrinsic value in it." He sees that it could be made a thing of beauty, and although it is in the rubbish heap it does not belong there. He finds out the price of the article and pays for it; then it is his, and it is sanctified; it is separated from the rubbish. That is what God did for me when He saved my soul. He came along and took me out of the rubbish heap, and He has done that for every redeemed sinner. I tell you we were sorry spectacles when He found us, and although we may have looked good to ourselves on the outside, we were unclean on the inside. One came my way and One came yours and when He saw us He loved us: He saw that we were worth buying, but oh, the price He paid! "Not redeemed with corruptible things, as silver and gold, but with the precious blood of Christ, as of a lamb without blemish and without spot." I praise God for the day that He put me on His shoulder and took me home rejoicing, and I said good-by to the rubbish heap; I was separated and set apart.

Let us go back to our picture: here is our friend coming home from the market place with the vessel under

His arm. What does He do as soon as He gets home? He begins to scrape it and clean it, and to hammer out some of the dents. After a time it looks so different, and when He has finished, it is shining and beautiful, and He puts it in a place of prominence—a thing of beauty. There you have the secondary thought of sanctification. I praise God that after He bought me with the precious blood, He started to work on me and began rubbing and cleaning me. Have you had any corners knocked off this week? It is all right; you are being sanctified.

As you study the Word of God, you will find there are three divine agencies which God uses to sanctify His people. The first of these three agencies is the blood; we receive the sanctification of the blood by faith. As the sinner plunges beneath the cleansing fountain by faith the blood washes him whiter than snow.

The second divine agency is the Word. Christ loved the church, as we read in Ephesians 5:26, and gave Himself for it, that He might sanctify it with the washing of water by the Word. In John 17:17 we read, "Sanctify them through thy truth: thy word is truth." I am sorry to say that there are many people who can sing and clap and jump when you mention the blood, but when you start talking to them about sanctification by the Word they take a look at their watch and are ready to go home. Many Pentecostal saints are not sanctified by the Word although they are by the blood. God baptized saints in the Holy Spirit because they were willing to be sanctified by the blood, but since then they have refused to be sanctified by the Word, and that is the root of most of the trouble in Pentecost today. The blood sanctifies us by faith, but the Word by obedience.

The third divine agency is the Spirit. When we start out to obey the Word, we find we have a job that is far too big for us, but what I cannot do, God comes and does for me, and while I walk in the fullness of the Spirit I obey the Word from my heart. But the trouble with so many is that they have lost the fullness of the Spirit. They have had the Baptism and love to talk about when the fire fell, but now they have lost the fullness, and because of that they have lost the victory. Therefore they are no longer being sanctified by the Word because they cannot obey it in their own strength.

We need all three forms of sanctification. Do you have them all? Have you a conscience void of offense because you plunged beneath the blood? Are you obeying the Word and are you filled with the Holy Spirit now and walking in the Spirit? If so, you are being sanctified and I congratulate you. Just remember that divine sanctification means a setting apart in principle from sin unto God through union with Christ; and when God has set you apart He proceeds to clean you up and for that He has three divine agencies; the blood, the Word and the Spirit.

Now I have finished speaking on God sanctifying you and I want to speak on you sanctifying yourself, the human end of sanctification. It is twofold. First of all we shall begin where we began before—with the Lord Jesus Christ. In John 17:19 we saw that God sanctified Him, but that was not sufficient; God could have sanctified Him and yet the scheme of redemption might have failed, but Jesus said, "I sanctify (set apart) myself." The two worked together and because of that, hell is defeated and I am saved. All Jesus' earthly life was a continual sanctifying of Himself to do the Father's will. Again and again the devil tried to make Him swerve from the path of obedience, but right through the Garden of Gethsemane and on through Calvary He sanctified Himself. "The cup which my Father hath given me to drink, shall I not drink it?" Yes, He drank it to the last dregs and because of my Savior's consecration, I am saved.

But I must proceed. You will see that our second line of thought is that man sanctifies himself. Let us study this a while. We are all called to be kings and priests. Ministers need to sanctify themselves. It is not enough that God has laid His hand upon us. When I was in San Francisco I came to the school one morning to have breakfast and I found all the young men, seventy or more, singing lustily in the full strength of their voices the chorus, "I know the Lord has Laid His Hand on Me." It was grand and the next time I lectured to them I mentioned how I had enjoyed their singing, but I reminded them that if the Lord had laid His hand upon them, there was something else needed and that was they should lay their hands upon themselves. Was I right? Many a man today has failed in the ministry, not because God didn't lay His hand upon him, but because that man failed to lay his hand upon himself. That is the reason the crash came. It is not enough for God to sanctify me; there can be failure even after that. Jeremiah and Paul might have been failures had they not sanctified themselves, and the horror of it was always before them. Oh that we might grip this truth!

Let me take you to the familiar story of the priest sanctifying himself. 2 Chronicles 29:5: "Hear me, ye Levites; sanctify now yourselves." And then let us read verse 34: "But the priests were too few, so that they could not flay all the burnt offerings: wherefore their brethren the Levites did help them, till the work was ended, and until the other priests had sanctified themselves: for the Levites were more upright in heart to sanctify themselves than the priests." May God save some of us in the ministry today from having to hide our faces in shame because some of the brethren who are not in the ministry are more sanctified than we have been. What a picture this is! God had sanctified the whole tribe of Levi, saying, "You shall not have any inheritance of the land. I am your possession." But the Levites had to sanctify *themselves,* and out of this tribe God had separated the house of Aaron, and the house of Aaron had to sanctify themselves.

If God has sanctified you, how urgent it is that you sanctify yourself. In 1 Corinthians 9:25, Paul who was sanctified from his birth, says, "And every man that striveth for the mastery is temperate in all things." And then speaking of the race of life he goes on to say, "But I keep under my body, and bring it into subjection; lest that by any means, when I have preached to others, I myself should be a castaway." That is Paul sanctifying himself. And that I might finish it I want you to remember his words to his son in the gospel, "If a man therefore purge himself from these, he shall be a vessel unto honor, sanctified, and meet for the Master's use, and prepared unto every good work" (2 Timothy 2:21). And verse 22: "Flee therefore youthful lusts; but follow righteousness, faith, charity, peace, with them that call on the Lord out of a pure heart." Many times I hear people praying, "O God, purge me, cleanse me!" and I sometimes think we need the strong words of Paul, *"Purge yourself."* We are asking God to do many things which He tells us to do for ourselves.

Always remember that there are two ends to sanctification. God's end is a finished work; I receive it in all its entirety, but God says, *"Sanctify yourself."* I realize that as a minister of the gospel I must have this worked out in my life before I can instruct others. The Grecian athletes had ten months of rigid training, but we have rigid training until we see Him face to face. Let me stop sanctifying myself for a week and the anointing begins to leave my ministry; let me lie down on any line and my ministry becomes poor and lifeless. May God help us who are ministers to sanctify ourselves. I know the Lord has laid His hand on me, and I thank God that He separated me for the gospel. When I gave up my business in London some of my friends said, "You are mistaken; God never called you to be a minister but a business man." But I knew He had called me, and today I know I am in the center of God's will and that He has given me a message for the Pentecostal people, for it is burning in my soul. But it is not sufficient to have a message burning in your soul. I can still preach to others and I myself become a castaway unless I respond to God's call to sanctify myself.

But I want to apply the truth to everyone, not only to the ministers. Let me say again, that if you are a believer God has sanctified you; He has washed you, but now you have to sanctify yourself. Are you ready to do this? I bring you back to 1 Corinthians 6:19, 20. If Paul had been around and heard some things I have heard coming into Christian homes over the air he would have thundered this out more than ever: "What! know ye not that your body is the temple of the Holy Ghost which is in you?" That old teaching that we are free from the law, is showing its head again. Yes, I am free from the law written on tables of stone, but I am not free from the law of God written in my heart. The fact that God has sanctified me is a supreme reason why I must sanctify myself. The apostle says, "Ye are washed, ye are sanctified," and then he further says, "Therefore, glorify God in your body and in your spirit which is God's." Because God has sanctified me I have a solemn responsibility to sanctify myself.

You will remember how when God wanted to speak to the children of Israel from Mount Sinai, He said to Moses, "On the third day I shall speak to the children of Israel. Tell them to sanctify themselves," and they did. There was a great cleaning up in the camp and on

the third day God drew near and spoke to sanctified
people who sanctified themselves. Again and again as I
travel around the world, people say to me, "Brother
Gee, God doesn't speak to me. I don't see things in the
Bible as some people do." I sometimes wonder if the
reason for this is that they haven't been sanctifying
themselves. I don't expect God to speak to a man from
the Bible when that man spends hours and hours reading the newspaper and five minutes in reading the
Word. I have been in Pentecostal homes where they will
listen to all sorts of things over the radio and then they
wonder why they do not hear God speak to them. You
cannot hear God speaking for the radio. I do not wish
to speak against the radio, for it can be a means of great
blessing, but it is like everything else; you have to have
it tremendously sanctified. I am not against an automobile but the automobile has to be sanctified. I am not
against recreation; we absolutely need it. Nevertheless,
recreation needs to be sanctified. May the Lord help us
to *sanctify ourselves* and if anyone is complaining because he has not heard God speak for a long while, let
me suggest that the failure might be right there. If you
sanctify yourself for three days you may hear His voice
again, and perhaps He will not keep you waiting that
long. You may even hear Him today.

There was another time when they sanctified themselves. God said to Joshua, "Sanctify the people, for I
shall do wonders amongst them." Isn't that what we
want God to do? We long to have God work wonders
among us. Today people say, "Let us get this famous
evangelist," and they think perhaps he will bring the
wonders in his suitcase. I believe the greatest necessity
in order to have Pentecost revived is sanctification. Remember that before God did signs and wonders the
people had to sanctify themselves. May God help us to
be in deep earnest about this blessed truth.

5

Is Our Modern Revival
Deep Enough?

This chapter will be devoted to the depth of our modern Pentecostal revival. Is it deep enough? Is the type of revival we are accustomed to today having a deep enough effect upon the lives of men and women? I feel very deeply stirred on this line, and it has been burning in my bones as I see conditions all over the world. I want us to consider Matthew 11:20: "Then began he to upbraid the cities wherein most of his mighty works were done, because they repented not."

First of all, I want to do justice to what God is doing among us, for I do thank God for all we have seen and rejoiced in; there is a glorious side to the revival which God is giving us. In many places we have seen that the modern revival is *breaking down the indifference,* and in some places the largest auditoriums have been necessary to accommodate the crowds that gather. We are finding that the gospel in its fullness has a grip upon men and women. We have found the dynamic power that is able to break down the indifference, and it has been a great privilege for me to travel around the world and see the marvelous grip which this revival has in so many countries.

When I visited Finland I was amazed to find thousands of Pentecostal people. In Sweden I found the great Filadelphia Church in Stockholm with five thousand members, and over in Norway we saw between eighteen hundred and two thousand people attending the meetings. Yes, I thank God for all that He is doing in this glorious revival.

I want to praise God that the revival we are now having is bringing back *a testimony to the supernatural,* for I am positive that God wants the church to have such a testimony. I thank God for the baptism in the Holy Spirit and for all it is bringing back of the supernatural in our personal experience. I glory in the supernatural part of this revival and I want to say to the Pentecostal people, if you let down on the supernatural you are failing God. If you can win the crowd only by letting down on the supernatural, beware of the crowd. May God help us to put Him first. I also want to thank God for all He has been doing in the way of divine healing.

And the next thing I rejoice over is that this glorious revival, this present modern Pentecostal revival, has brought *a deep satisfaction* in the Christian experience of many believers who at one time were unsatisfied. I was moved by the testimony of a man who said that he had been a Christian for years but had been unsatisfied and groping around, but now the Lord had baptized him and his wife in the Holy Ghost and they were satisfied.

So I rejoice in a Christ that satisfies my heart; I am rejoicing in an experience that satisfies the longing of the soul. I do not mean that I have all there is to get, but I am rejoicing in an "unsatisfied satisfaction." Yes, we have found in this revival the weapon that conquers indifference and we have seen it bringing back to the church some measure of the supernatural. The consequence is that the dominant note wherever I go is that of joy, and the dominant feature of our meetings is singing. Oh, we are a singing crowd! We cannot help it, for we have the song in our hearts. May the Lord keep the joy and the song ever with us, for it is attractive to a weary world. But having said all this, I want to repeat my question:

Is the Modern Revival Deep Enough?

When I get home from meetings I usually do some thinking. And when I settle down before God and think over these things which have stirred my heart very deeply, I ask myself this question more and more. The more I see the more the question forces itself upon me: Is our modern revival deep enough? There are three question marks on my heart, and the first question mark is on the line of shallowness. Everywhere I go I find indications of shallowness; I find the modern revival is very bright and happy, but I fear it is also very shallow, and I am very concerned about that because I do not believe that which satisfies the heart of God is shallow. God is working for eternity, and when I find shallowness I am afraid of the consequences. I may be wrong, but one of the things I find in the modern revival is a great tendency to get the congregation happy and get them all singing and smiling and the general slogan of the modern evangelist seems to be, "Are you happy? Everybody happy?" He wants them to say "Amen," and so he drills them in this, and for the first two or three nights everyone shouts, "Amen."

If I understand my Bible, a real revival begins by making everyone unhappy. Real happiness begins with unhappiness where sinners are concerned. The mighty revivals of our fathers' days used to make congregations weep instead of laugh. I am not sure that we are right in asking a congregation containing sinners, whether everyone is happy. They ought not to be happy. No, I am afraid we are suffering from too much shallowness.

I feel the same way about our baptisms in the Holy Spirit; they seem shallow. I have seen young people, almost immediately after they get up from their knees, talk about the most frivolous things. I do not believe that if you have a real infilling of the Holy Spirit you will behave like that; the genuine Baptism leaves you for days as if you were walking in another world, and it takes you some time to get adjusted. The real Baptism makes an indelible impression on your life. Some of us received the real thing in days gone by, and we are anxious to see others getting the same today.

Another thing that convinces me that we are too shallow today is the behavior both before and after our services. As I have been traveling all over the world, one of the things that grieves me in so many places is the buzz of conversation that goes on right up till the song leader announces the first song. I fear we have lost the sense of the presence of God. I always remember what an elder of my church in Edinburgh said to me one time. I found that my church was one buzz of conversation before the meeting began, and it grieved me so that I prayed about it in the service. It was then that this elder said to me, "I agree with you, but I got so tired of the frozen attitude of the Presbyterian Church that when I came into Pentecost I was glad to feel the free spirit." I am not advocating a freezing atmosphere; by all means let us keep that family spirit, but let us remember that our great Father is in our midst. I was brought up from childhood to bow my head in a few moments of silent prayer when I first entered the house of God, and I wish we all might have that habit now.

But if the behavior before the service troubles me, the behavior after the service is of still greater concern. The place seems to be one roar of conversation as soon as the meeting is dismissed. In some places where we have had a stream of people at the altar, some seeking salvation and others the Baptism, you could hardly collect your thoughts enough to pray for the seekers because of the buzz of conversation going on in the audience. It shows a shallowness somewhere. Oh, that we might come back to a sense of awe and wonder when God is working! I think of some glorious times when God has been baptizing in the Holy Spirit when others who were privileged to be present would feel the presence of the Lord so that they wanted to take their shoes off their feet!

Another thing that concerns me is the *easy backsliding* today. I am afraid it is because they come in quickly that they go out so quickly. If you get a thing cheaply you don't appreciate it very much, but if you pay a price for it, it is exceedingly precious. While in California recently I was privileged to have dinner with a Japanese brother, now a sincere Christian. He opened up his heart to me that night and said, "You know I am seeking the baptism in the Holy Spirit, but time and time again I have been tempted to have nothing to do with the Pentecostal people because I have been so distressed over the levity which I have seen in their meetings. But while I have seen all that, I realize that God is in the movement." Then he continued, "You know I am a wholesale china merchant and I find that I can buy up the cheap china in great quantities and sell it again as quickly as I buy it, but when I have a very choice piece of china, something that I have taken great trouble to get, it sometimes takes me months to sell that. I feel that is the way with your people. I may take a little longer and go slower, and it may take a deeper work, but quality always pays in the long run." Friends, my Pentecost cost me something, but I find every time, that which takes time is more precious. Let us beware of that which is shallow. So the first question mark in my heart is this shallowness which I see everywhere, and it makes me pray, "O Lord, do a deeper work, and if it is to begin with the preachers (and I believe it is), then, Lord, make it begin with them."

The next thing that puts a question mark in my heart, I scarcely like to mention, but just here I am using great plainness of speech. It is the lack of holiness, which is most deplorable. I have found that in the last few months God has been giving me to speak often on the subject of *Sanctification,* and people welcome it and thank God for it. I am rather concerned about this habit we have of always presenting the gospel in a fourfold way. Dr. A. B. Simpson started it and in his four essentials he left out the baptism in the Holy Spirit. We have picked up the slogan, have put in the Baptism, but unfortunately we have left out sanctification. Let me say that I should rather have a fivefold gospel and include sanctification than a fourfold gospel without it. Oh, the tragedies we have seen because of the lack of holiness! Mighty men of God right in the forefront of the battle are falling! May the Lord give us an increase of holiness; for my part a revival that does not produce holiness does not go deep enough.

The third question mark in my heart concerning the modern revival, and that which is giving me the gravest concern, is the *waning of the supernatural.* Although God sent this revival to start the supernatural, the supernatural is getting less and less. I was in a camp meeting some time ago where God graciously met us in old-time power. A young woman in that meeting who had been in Pentecostal work for eighteen months, said. "That is the first time I have heard a message in tongues with the interpretation." I went to another revival and the Spirit of God came upon a brother minister and myself and we had prophecy with tongues and interpreta-

tion and the pastor of that assembly took me into his office and said, "Brother Gee, we haven't had that happen
in this church for over two years." I could give other
like instances. You can imagine that I was full of praise
to God when in a large Bible School recently I found
real Pentecost. May God keep "Pentecost" Pentecostal.
I firmly believe that we must have a manifestation of the
Spirit of God among us. I find everywhere that the
meetings are running into a rut; we start with three
hymns, then we have requests for prayer, and the whole
thing runs according to program; but in a real, live,
Pentecostal church we should never know what will
take place next! There is order, but there is also *life* and
that infinite variety that always marks the work of God.
A real Pentecostal meeting is nothing less than the gate
of heaven.

What I grieve for most of all is our young people who
have never seen what we older ones have seen. We can
remember the days of twenty years ago, but our young
people haven't had that privilege. As I go around from
one Bible school to another and face our solid ranks of
young people, I pray that God will help me to put the
vision before them. So many have no vision of real
"Pentecost." I feel I can do without choirs or orches-
tras, but give me back the old anointings.

If you were to ask me what I believe to be the deepest need among us, I would say that *the deepest need
of every revival is repentance*. If repentance is not in a
revival, it does not go deep enough.

Read again the verse used in the opening paragraph
of this chapter: "Then began he to upbraid the cities
where most of his mighty works were done, because
they repented not." There must be repentance before
there can be a real revival. I am afraid that in our modern revivals we are missing God's first word to sinners.
His first word to them is not "believe," but *"repent."*

Am I right? When John the Baptist came to preach, his first word was *"repent";* when the Lord Jesus began His ministry His first word was *"repent."* When He gave that matchless picture of the Prodigal Son, it becomes blacker and blacker until at last the young man comes to himself, and he says, "I will arise and go to my father." His father never moved a step to meet him until the son took the first step. Repentance came first. On the Day of Pentecost, under the fresh fire of the Spirit of God, Peter's first word to their inquiry what they should do, was "Repent and be baptized." Repentance is the prerequisite of the baptism in the Holy Spirit. I am wondering if that is not why some of our present-day Baptisms are so shallow—lack of repentance.

If we do not repent, what is the alternative? We will presume that we will do without repentance. If you do away with repentance—which is a change of the mind and the heart toward sin—the alternative is that men's hearts will not be broken; they will not be touched nor moved; hence it will be a superficial work.

The Lord Jesus gave us a picture for all time of a revival without repentance in His Parable of the Sower. There was stony ground that had not been broken up. Read the significant picture in Matthew 13, verse 5, and then notice verses 20 and 21, where He gives us an interpretation of His own parable. The man had lost his joy. He had received the seed with joy but when tribulation came along he fell by the wayside. These stony-ground people receive the gospel with joy; they love to sing and clap their hands and they say, "Oh, this is wonderful!" They receive it with joy, but the Lord says, "They have no root." Then He said that when tribulation and persecution come, they fail to stand up under it. My friends, we are having sunshine more or less now, but I want to warn you that tribulation is coming. Over in Europe we are a little closer to it than you are in America, but it will come here also. Last March my wife and I traveled right to the frontier of Soviet Russia, and I have been so near that we could hear the rumblings; and tonight, while we sit comfortably in this church, our Pentecostal brethren are suffering in prison. But we don't have to wait for that; we read of tribulation received because of the Word. Let a real preacher preach the Word and you will soon see a thinning out process begin. You can always get a crowd when you stoop to psychological methods, but when you begin giving the strong Word of God you will often see the crowd sifting down.

A beautiful thing about people who have repented is that they love the Word. The more the Word searches the more they love it. A few weeks ago a dear woman in the meeting began to scream and cry out just as soon as the service closed. I gave a little teaching that we didn't need to do things like that when it was not of the Holy Spirit but just our own doings. On my last evening in that city that woman came and shook hands with me and said, "Mr. Gee, I do thank God for what you said. I see that I was wrong, and I am so grateful to you for putting me right; I appreciate the teaching with all my heart." Would God that we had more of that spirit. So often we find people getting offended and then they run off to some other church. If you do that, you have never repented as you should.

Our Lord could see what was ahead; He knew that the sunshine wouldn't always last, He knew that persecution was sure to come, and He was anxious that those to whom He was preaching in the sunshine would get established so that they would stand when troubles came. I have been through two wars, and I shall never forget those days of agony. We do not know when the next and a worse one will come, and I am asking God to help me to make the most of the sunshine. I do not know how long it will be before the highways of the world will be closed, so I want to make the most of my time. Let us learn to find the way in the light and then we will know it in the dark; learn to trust God, while it is yet easy, and when the storm breaks it will be instinctive.

Now I want to be constructive in a few words, showing how we can have a revival of repentance. What methods may we adopt to bring about a deeper work? I have been able to interest people and hold my congregations, and people kindly come and say. "Brother Gee, you have been a help to us." But let me say that doesn't satisfy. The thing that distresses me is that under my ministry I do not see more men and women broken down; I want to see them weeping, and I am praying that God will give me a greater anointing of the Spirit. One of the most delightful experiences in Finland took place in one of the midday Bible studies. A roughly dressed man whose burly young son had driven in from the farm was present. The old man was covered with the soil of the country, but he loved to hear the Word. I remember how he came stumbling to the front to kneel at the altar. I didn't understand his language, so was unable to talk with him, but some of the brethren helped him, and after a few moments he got up and there, where he had knelt, was a puddle of tears and the old man's face was shining with the glory of God. I said, "O God, give me more of that."

How can we have a revival of repentance? I believe three things are necessary for this. We need more solid preaching of judgment to come. "Oh," you say, "you are old-fashioned." If there is a judgment seat there can be nothing old-fashioned about preaching it. Our Lord Jesus wept over cities because they did not repent, because He had a vision of the judgment seat, and He said that in the judgment it would be better for Sodom and

Gomorrah than for them. We do not hear much about the judgment seat today; they prefer to talk about universal salvation. But let me add that there is not only a judgment for sinners, but also a judgment seat of Christ for believers; there is a place where my work will be tested, the wood and the stubble will be burned, but the gold and silver will remain. Oh, for more preaching along this line! But our preachers will never preach it until they tremble before the judgment seat themselves.

Second, if we want repentance, we are absolutely helpless until the Holy Spirit gives it. I am Calvinistic enough in my theology to believe that it is the Spirit of God that moves men to repentance, and unless the Lord moves, they will not repent. But I believe that the Spirit of God is ever ready to move men to repentance. If you preach without the Spirit of God, you will soon make men hard, so our greatest need is the blessed Holy Spirit. If the ground has to be broken up, you have to have more than a shower: you must have rain from heaven. I remember the old farm in England and how in the hot, scorching summer the time came when we couldn't even plough the ground; it was not till we had a fresh shower of rain that we could put the plowshare in. Friends, even our plowing with the Word is vain until we have a fresh shower from heaven. O God, send us the showers! "Ask ye of the Lord rain in the time of the latter rain." Preaching alone will never give the desired result. We need showers of heavenly grace. I trust you will take this message on your hearts and pray that God will pour out His Spirit once again.

While we are dependent upon the Spirit of God, I do believe that God will use and bless an anointed ministry. Is there not a vast difference between a gifted ministry and an anointed ministry? Some preachers dazzle men by their gifts, but that is not an anointing. Oh, I am hungry to see an anointed ministry! A ministry that produces repentance because the preachers have seen the King, the Lord of hosts, and they have realized in His spotless, shining presence what sin is. When a man comes out from that presence he comes out with something resting upon him that brings the grace of the Lord upon the people.

Let us pray for a fresh outpouring of the Holy Spirit upon the preacher and upon everyone of us until the ground is softened by the "latter rain" and until we get a deeper revival, a revival that produces repentance, and after it has produced that will keep us broken, melted, and softened before the Lord.

6

How the Church Grew

There are many passages in the Book of Acts showing the amazing miracle of church growth. The following verses will give you a picture of that amazing growth. First, Acts 1:15: "And in those days Peter stood up in the midst of the disciples . . . (the number of names together were *about an hundred and twenty*)." Acts 2:41: "Then they that gladly received his word were baptized; and the same day there were added unto them *about three thousand souls*." Acts 2:47: "And the Lord *added to the church daily* such as should be saved." Acts 4:4: "Howbeit many of them which heard the word believed; and the number of men was *about five thousand*." Acts 5:14: "And believers were the more *added* to the Lord, *multitudes* both men and women." Acts 6:7: "And the word of God increased;

and the number of the disciples multiplied in Jerusalem greatly; and a *great company of the priests* were obedient to the faith." Acts 9:31: "Then had the churches rest throughout all Judea and Galilee and Samaria, and were edified; and walking in the fear of the Lord, and in the comfort of the Holy Ghost, *were multiplied.*"

I could refer you to many more passages showing that amazing miracle of history—the growth of the early church—but we have taken quite as much as we can get through for this chapter. I want you to study with me this marvelous thing and you will see that underlying every new step of growth there is a principle, and that principle will be a secret for us to learn so that we can see how the church of God can grow in our day.

When I first came into this Pentecostal movement some of us had the idea that what the Lord wanted us to do was to hide ourselves away in little back missions, just get together and get ready for the coming of the Lord. We fondly thought ourselves to be little jugs of spiritual cream. And we had lovely little Bible talks in Mrs. So-and-So's drawing room—all of us getting ready for the coming of the Lord. And it didn't seem to matter to us that while twenty-five of us could be in some drawing room having lovely little Bible talks that twenty-five thousand sinners could be outside going to hell, But thank God, we got over that and we are growing. We are more scriptural, and I thank God we have a burning passion to grow and grow and grow. There was a day when I thought a small gathering was the very essence of delight; today the bigger the meeting the better I like it.

Jesus is such a wonderful Savior that we want everybody to know about it. And then there's the baptism with the Holy Spirit. It is such a marvelous experience for the Christian that we want everyone to have it. My desire is that we may grow exceedingly. Lord, give us the vision of growth!

First. Now we'll begin with the hundred and twenty people in the upper room praying. Acts 1:15. Only one hundred and twenty, but thank God that hundred and twenty were living seed from which was going to grow the church of the living God. They were *praying* and every *real* growth always begins with people praying. If you want to see spiritual growth you have to do something more than get gifted preachers and gifted musicians and more than large audiences. Real growth begins with a company of consecrated people praying. The root of every revival is in prayer. The root of every Pentecost is prayer. God save us from thinking that anything can ever take the place of prayer. The first step of growth began because the seed of the church was steeped in *prayer*.

Second. The next mighty growth is in Acts 2:41: "Then they that gladly received his word were baptized: and the same day there were added unto them about three thousand souls." That was a good growth—one hundred and twenty to three thousand. What produced this? I need not tell a Pentecostal group what produced it. The thing that produced "*this*" was "*that!*" (Acts 2:16). Hallelujah! In answer to believing prayer the heavens were opened and the Spirit of God descended upon them. Now, I am not talking so much about growth in membership. People are added to the church when there is a fresh Pentecostal outpouring of the Spirit. Every section of God's true church needs a new enduement of power from on high. We must have another Pentecost, and I greatly deplore the narrowing down of the vision of our beloved Pentecostal people. Some of our people are becoming denominational. May God make us bigger. I can't be satisfied with this wonderful Baptism just for myself. The whole Church needs it. God keep us with big hearts and big vision. "We need another Pentecost; send the fire!"

I had the privilege of attending one of the centenary meetings of the founder of the China Inland Mission— Hudson Taylor. I was greatly moved by what Dr. Howard Taylor, Hudson Taylor's son, said: "I am speaking about the tremendous challenge of the races yet unevangelized—the multitudes still waiting to hear the words of life. It seems to me that unless the Church receives some new dynamic from on high, we shall never be able to undertake the task that lies in front of us."

I thank God that we know what that dynamic from on high is. Let us be true to Pentecost. We have the message of the hour. People sometimes find fault with us in this movement because we get a little bit enthusiastic. I plead guilty. It is a good thing to get enthusiastic about religion. When I was in Minneapolis one afternoon we switched on the radio to the big political convention in Chicago. The one thing I noticed was that if I ever heard enthusiasm, I surely heard it then. They were shouting and shouting until it nearly burst the radio. And when I heard them shouting I thought, "Well, what's wrong with us when we get a little bit like that over religion?" A little dose of enthusiasm would do our churches good.

If you really go to the root of that word enthusiasm, it means getting a little overheated. You can choose between the two, but as for me I should rather be a little overheated than frozen up. If your engine gets a little heated up because you have been climbing, you can stop and cool it off, while you enjoy the view. I know there is danger in fanaticism but I'd rather have a little bit too much fire than to be frozen up. We have discovered these days how to deal with people who get too hot. You only have to throw a little bit of this water (the Bible) on them!

So we see the second growth was produced by the baptism in the Holy Spirit and fire. We shall never grow very much until we have had the Baptism.

Third. The third growth we see in Acts 2:47: "And the Lord added to the church daily such as should be saved." This is my idea of healthy growth, when the Lord is adding to the church regularly all the time. Some assemblies grow only when they have a special evangelist. I think the best assemblies are those that are growing all of the time. Don't misunderstand me. I thank God for the evangelists, but, nevertheless, I love those assemblies where the whole life of the assembly is so healthy, where the people are so full of the passion for souls, that souls are being born again all of the time. The best way to grow is not by jerks, but steadily. "The Lord added to the church daily." This happened because the church was healthy. Real healthy assemblies are having spiritual children born in their midst all of the time. In verse 46 of this same chapter we read, "And they, continuing daily with one accord in the temple, and breaking bread from house to house, did eat their meat with gladness and singleness of heart, praising God, and having favor with all the people." I think the principal keynote of the condition of the church here that made it healthy and enabled the Lord to add to it daily was unity of heart. Unity is an essential thing, the keynote of growth. The unity here was unity of heart. Some of our brethren are fighting for unity of doctrine. The older I get the more tolerant I become, and the more I see that there are very few absolute essentials. Lots of things that we make issues of we shall blush about when we come before the judgment seat of Christ. God make us bigger.

I find some assemblies splitting up over small points of doctrine, such as whether the church will go through the tribulation or not, and starting new assemblies that refuse to fellowship one another. If you want to go through the tribulation you are welcome. I am not going to disfellowship you if you want to do so. Oh, the wretched things that we make issues of! You can quarrel about these things if you like, but when you are in the front line fox holes you haven't time for them. If you meet a Christian there you are not much bothered about the particular brand he is.

One afternoon I was in a little town in Asia where there were only two missions, one Pentecostal, the other Episcopal. As soon as I got there a beautiful young missionary from the Episcopal mission, a Fundamentalist, a young graduate just out from Cambridge, knocked at our door. He gripped my hand and thanked God I was there. And did I freeze him because he happened to be something else besides Pentecostal? We were surrounded by inky blackness of Mohammedanism. He said, "Brother Gee, thank God you have come." God forgive us for being so pitifully small. Gypsy Smith said, "Some people are not sectarian—they are *insectarian.*"

It is unity of heart that makes us grow. Once I was in a glorious Pentecostal convention. The Lord was having His way, and I remember one morning the Spirit of God came on the sister who was hostess of the convention. She walked up and down and praised the Lord, and the Lord gave us a wonderful prophecy through her lips. I shall never forget the burden of that prophetic message, "You will never unite the people with the doctrine, but you will with the glory."

In the prayer of our Lord Jesus we find these words in John 17:22, "*And the glory which thou gavest me I have given them; that they may be one, even as we are one.*" The thing that makes us one is the glory. On that platform behind me I had such a mixture of doctrine that I should have got almost dizzy sorting them all out, but the glory united us. Some people don't agree with me on points of doctrine, but if we get soaked up with the glory we get on fine. If you think I'm not right on doctrine, give me the chapter and verse and the next place I'll put it right. The thing I am after is that we shall be enveloped in the glory of the Lord.

Fourth. The next growth is in Acts 4:4, "Howbeit many of them which heard the word believed; and the number of the men was about five thousand." Another big growth! What produced this? It was the Word; they heard the Word. They believed the Word and they became about five thousand. We'll never grow without the preaching of the Word of God. Never! God give us more of the Word. We need to be filled with the Spirit and we also need to be filled with the Word. The trouble with many of us is that we have been filled with the Spirit, but we haven't paid enough attention to being filled with the Word. That is why we haven't grown. You can't grow on only tongues and interpretations and visions. The thing that makes us grow is the Word.

The Word that produced the growth here was the Word about Jesus. In chapters two and three all the burden of their preaching was Jesus, Jesus, Jesus! What are we doing, brethren, when we make mountains out of molehills! God has sent us into the world to preach Christ, and the baptism in the Holy Spirit is to make us flaming preachers of Christ. You are on the wrong track when you are preaching all these hobbies. Quit them and preach Christ! Some people make a hobby of the coming of the Lord, of divine healing, or of gifts of the Spirit. Don't make a hobby even of Pentecost. Preach Christ! All these things are a very blessed part of the gospel but we must preach Jesus Himself. Many preachers of holiness talk so much about short skirts. All they can preach about is stuff like that. Have you never heard, "*He* is made unto us sanctification"? The best preaching of holiness is the preaching of Christ. You can preach about short skirts and all this sort of thing in the flesh. You don't need much anointing to do that. But when you preach Christ you need the anointing of the Spirit.

> What the world needs is Jesus,
>   Just a glimpse of Him.
> He will bring joy and gladness,
>   Take away sin and sadness.
> What the world needs is Jesus,
>   Just a glimpse of Him.

We are all needing Jesus. Hallelujah! The Lord give us to be great preachers of CHRIST. That is what added to the church.

Why is it that the Pentecostal movement is holding on in such mighty victory? Because, thank God, we are clearing off all the trimmings and trappings and we are coming to the big thing and we are preaching Christ.

Fifth. Now the next thing that produced growth, Acts 5:14, "And believers were the more added to the Lord, multitudes both of men and women." Now I want you to notice that the things that preceded this growth was the tragic incident of Ananias and Sapphira. There was a cleaning up and after the cleaning up the church grew again. When I was in a great General Council meeting in England just before I came to America, a preacher announced his text from the second chapter of Acts. From all over the crowd came Amen, Praise the Lord, etc. A few days later the same preacher got up and announced his text from the fifth chapter of Acts, and you could have heard a pin drop. The book of Acts has a fifth chapter as well as a second, and we might occasionally preach a very solemn sermon from the fifth chapter.

It was a dramatic and terrible scene. Ananias and

Sapphira had agreed together that they would try a little experiment on the Spirit of the Lord. They didn't like Peter very much and they said, "I don't believe that he is as full of the Holy Spirit as he pretends to be. Let's try a little trick on him. We'll sell that land and we won't say how much we have got for it, and we'll pretend that we are giving the whole amount but we'll only give a small part. We'll get the glory for giving the whole price and we can spend the change."

So they decided on this deceit. Ananias came into the assembly and brought part of the price of the possession, and laid it at the disciples' feet. And Peter full of the Holy Spirit saw through the whole thing like a flash. He said, "Did you sell it for so much?" "Yes," telling a brazen lie in the presence of God. Then Peter became transformed for the time being into a man of steel. Mark you, there comes a time in the church of God when the leaders need to be transformed into leaders of steel. This is the loving, emotional Peter who was delighted to say to the man at the temple gate, "Silver and gold have I none; but such as I have give I thee; In the name of Jesus Christ of Nazareth rise up and walk." That very man who was so full of the love of God, when it came to a need of cleansing, was transformed into a man of steel. He said to Ananias, "While it was thine own, couldn't you do with it as you pleased? Why are you trying to bring this lie into the church of God?" I see the man turn ashy pale. I see him reel. There is a clash. He falls to the ground. His eyelids flicker. Then there is a corpse. A solemn hush comes over the people like the silence of death. It was a tremendous thing to belong to the church! The young men carried him out and buried him.

A few hours later his wife, Sapphira, came in, not knowing what had happened. As soon as she came in the door I can see a tightness grip the throat of everybody. Sapphira came up immediately to Peter. Now Peter is the judge upon the bench, a man of rock because holiness and revival—the life of the church—and the honor of God are at stake. "Tell me, did you sell that land for so much?" "Yes, so much." "How is it that ye have agreed together to try this experiment? The feet of those who have buried thy husband are at the door and shall carry thee out." The woman grew deathly pale. She dropped to the ground, a few convulsions, and she was dead. The young men picked her up and carried her out amid a hush that was as solemn as eternity, and buried her by her husband.

But you say, "Brother Gee, that sort of thing happened under the law." Yes, but this was *under grace*. You say, "But that sort of thing happened in the Old Testament." But this happened in the New Testament. You say, "That sort of thing happened before Calvary." This happened *after Calvary*. You say, "That sort of thing happened before Pentecost." This happened *after Pentecost*. I don't know one single dispensational reason why that couldn't happen in our meetings today. I sometimes think that it is only the mercy of God that lets some of us get out of a meeting alive instead of dead. It is a solemn thing to belong to the church of God.

My brethren, it is holiness that we must have before we grow. Let us never deceive ourselves into thinking that a revival can go on without holiness. Any revival that lets down on holiness is doomed. You can dig a grave, for before very long you will have to bury it. "Though I speak with the tongues of men and angels, and have not love, I am become as sounding brass, or a tinkling cymbal." You think you can have holiness by increasing the missionary offering! "Though I bestow all my goods to feed the poor, and though I give my body to be burned, and have not love, it profiteth me nothing." You think you can have holiness by increasing your training and preaching, "Though I have all knowledge and have not love . . . I am nothing." I do thank God that He is showing us that if we are going to have revival, we must have holiness.

I want to say to you that when the need comes in the church of God for the exercising of church discipline, please, in the name of Christ, don't make it harder for your leaders by turning around and criticizing them and say they ought to have more love. Remember Peter. One of the most lovely things in that story is that after it was all over I don't hear one word of murmuring and complaint. I don't hear, "Peter, you ought to have had more love. Let's turn him out and get another preacher." They recognized that the leaders were responsible for the holiness in the camp. But we do read (v. 12) that they were all with one accord in Solomon's porch. This blessed unity was not broken by critics.

I am one of the executive presbyters of the General Council in Great Britain, and one of the hardest things we have to do is to discipline a preacher who has failed God. When a preacher has failed on the moral line, and the only thing we can do is to discipline him, God knows we do it with broken hearts. And then the people turn around and say we should have had more love and that we only did it because we were jealous of him. God help us to obey them that have the rule over us. It is time for us to have discipline in the army of the Lord. Unless we have it we cannot advance. I do stand for Pentecostal leadership (Hebrews 13:17).

Do you know that in some European countries like Finland every week they have a church meeting for members only and admission is by ticket? When I go there they grant me the privilege of going. I can tell you they are meetings in which the power falls, because if you backslide your ticket is taken away from you. I shall never forget a meeting I was in where a sister was having to be put out of the assembly—a sister who had sinned morally. The consequence was that the testimony of the assembly was at stake. They pleaded with her to repent, but she refused to humble herself. The only thing they could do was to put her away from themselves. I personally believe in a membership roll, for unless you have one I don't see how you can tell who is yourself and who isn't. How can you put away from yourselves the wicked person when you don't know who is yourself and who isn't? (1 Corinthians 5:13).

They got up and explained the case. They said that there was no other course; they had tried everything else. She would have to be put away from the membership. Never will I forget that meeting. Those people are so intensely earnest. Oh, the groan and cry that went up from the congregation that God would bring that woman to repentance! If you had been there when they officially and publicly put her out of that church you would have thought you were back again in the New Testament. God give us church discipline!

Notice what happened to the early church after this. In verse 11 we read, "And great *fear* came upon all the church, and upon as many as heard these things." Fear and grace are the things we need. Will you misunderstand me if I say I think people can become too gracious? You can be so gracious that you are sticky with it. God knows we need a little bit of fear to balance. Some people have so much grace that it doesn't matter to them if someone brings dishonor to the name of Christ. You ought to have more fear. Some people are so gracious that they are even wanting to find a way to get the devil into heaven. What we need is not only grace but some fear along with it, some godly, holy fear —the sort of fear that made Noah build the ark—the sort of fear that makes us realize that it is a fearful thing to fall into the hands of the living God.

Some people say, "But Brother Gee, if we raise the standard as high as that nobody will join us." Why there are flocks just waiting for you to raise the standard. Because you don't is just the reason they don't join. I solemnly believe that there are thousands who would love to join us if we were more holy. Holiness attracts people.

When I was a young, struggling pastor in Edinburgh I did so want to see my church grow, and in my anxiety to see it grow I am ashamed to say that I admitted to the membership some who were not worthy. Didn't I suffer for it? They were a constant trouble ever afterwards. Didn't I learn my lesson? Don't lower your standard to get in some person just because he happens to be a rich banker. It was when the people had great fear that multitudes both of men and women were added to them. If we stand for holiness we may lose a few people at the beginning, but it will be worthwhile.

Sixth. Now chapter 6:7, "And the word of God increased; and the number of the disciples multiplied in Jerusalem greatly; and a great company of the priests were obedient to the faith."

What did it this time? Organization! Some people think organization is of the devil. God help them. I read in verse one, "And in those days, when the number of the disciples was multiplied, there arose a murmuring of the Grecians against the Hebrews, because their widows were neglected in the daily ministration." That's when the trouble happened, "when the number of the disciples were multiplied." You can't run a thing the same way when it is multiplied as you did when it was beginning. You can take it from the Word of God that when a thing grows you are going to have troubles that you won't have when it is smaller. Don't be so silly and sentimental as to be always wanting the old days back when there were only a handful and very few troubles. Some people can't bear big meetings because there is likely to be trouble in them.

Now because there was trouble they dealt with it. Some folks say, "Let's just pray and preach and forget about it." No. Get it by the scruff of the neck and deal with it. Don't run away from it. Be a man and face it. The twelve called the multitude of the disciples together. That was an act of courage. They "faced the music." Then they said, "It is not *reason* that we should leave the word of God, and serve tables." Reason is what we need sometimes. We need a lot more reason in Pentecost. Our testimony has suffered in many places because it has not been presented reasonably. God help us to be reasonable.

"Look ye out among you seven men of honest report, full of the Holy Ghost and wisdom, whom we may appoint over this business. But we will give ourselves continually to prayer, and to the ministry of the Word. And the saying pleased the whole multitude." The Church did its first bit of organizing and it saved the revival. Let's pull this "dragon" out and have a look at it. When you start talking about organization some people nearly faint. This is the principle: *It is always right to organize sufficiently to meet a felt need.* That is the principle. Have you got it? I know organization is a dangerous thing. I know that organization can kill revival. When they first organized the Assemblies of God I would not touch it, but the Lord cured me. I am just as free as any man in the Assemblies, and I have the benefit of being checked up by my brothers and sisters.

Organization is a deadly thing when you go beyond the need. The sort of men I am afraid of in the church are those who love organization for organization's sake. Some men are made that way. They love organizing everything. If you go into their offices you can see that everything is in its place. They usually can organize everything but their wife. They can't manage her. They love talking and discussing matters and they simply gloat in resolutions and two thirds majorities, etc. They are the men who do the mischief. Chain those fellows up and don't let them out till we are through with the business meeting. If you organize for the love of it you will kill the revival.

Organize only enough to meet a felt need. From 1906-1924 we had no Pentecostal Movement to speak of in Great Britain, but since we have organized the work has grown by leaps and bounds. There were two reasons why we organized. Before we organized we were being simply swamped by false doctrines and false preachers. Now we demand a certificate of fellowship. If you are thinking of going to Great Britain to preach, be sure to take along your certificate. The first thing we'll ask you for will be your credentials. Take my advice and stay here if you haven't credentials. We have to safeguard the church that God has put in our charge.

The other thing that we were longing to do was to put on a bigger missionary program and to get out a good paper and a song book. Unless we got together we couldn't do these things and they were becoming urgent needs. Now our missionary work is growing. We have more missionaries on the field than we ever had. God is blessing Scriptural organization. When it is meeting a need, organization is Scriptural and right. If you won't organize, your revival will explode and go to pieces.

Seventh. Now Acts 9:31 is a nice one to finish up on. "Then had the churches rest throughout all Judea and Galilee and Samaria, and were edified; and walking in the fear of the Lord, and in the comfort of the Holy Ghost, were multiplied."

I do say this that first of all you must have peace in

the assembly if you are going to grow. There must be peace. If there isn't peace in your assembly, drop everything else and get down before God and get peace in the assembly. It is no good asking our evangelists to come and expect them to bring a revival until you have peace in your midst. The Lord help us to see that we must have peace in our churches. If you are having a lot of spiritual gifts that are only producing trouble, they are not of the Spirit. "For ye may all prophesy one by one, that all may learn, and all may be comforted. And the spirits of the prophets are subject to the prophets. For God is not the author of confusion, *but of peace*. Real prophesying in the Spirit brings the peace of God in our midst; and if you have a brother or sister in your assembly whose spiritual gifts do not bring peace, mark that man or woman. Real gifts of the Spirit bring peace. If your gifts are making you a nuisance everywhere you go, I think you had better stop and see where your gifts are coming from. Ask some of the brethren to have a look at them with you.

My hope is that He will help us to make the most of our golden opportunities these days. If ever there was a time to give to missions it is now. The time may come when there will be no need. God forgive us for quarreling over details when we ought to be making the most of our opportunities. Preach, for the night cometh when no man can work!

7

The Tragedy of Sinning Against Light

"Know ye not that there is a prince and a great man fallen this day in Israel?"

I speak about the man who knew God's will but opposed it. That man is Abner, the captain of Saul's host, one of the tragedies of history. The highlights of the story we shall consider are found in the following references: 2 Samuel 2:4, 8-12; 3:8-12, 17-22, 26-28, 38. You are familiar with the delightful romance of how God brought David to the throne. How we love the story of Samuel's coming and anointing the shepherd lad before his brethren to be king over Israel; and then in the events that followed it seemed he could never be king.

For years David was being chased over the mountains until he himself said he was hunted like a partridge. It seemed impossible in the natural that David, twenty-six or twenty-seven years of age, could ever come to the throne; but when God promises a thing, He keeps His Word. God had said that David should reign over Israel and neither Saul nor anyone else could keep him off the throne. The time came when David was on the verge of ascending the promised throne, and Abner provided the last incident before that happened. Abner's part was sordid. When Saul committed suicide David was immediately hailed as king by the tribe of

Judah, and he set up his throne. Abner refused allegiance to David, but took one of Saul's sons and put him on the throne of Israel and kept him there by sheer force of arms. But after one or two years a little difference came up between them concerning a woman, and the result was that Abner went off in a furious temper, saying, "All right. I will teach you not to talk to me like that. I will turn the kingdom over to David." So he went down to David who received him courteously. I want you to notice the significant words of Abner: "For the Lord hath spoken of David, saying, By the hand of my servant David will I save my people Israel." The thing seems all settled, but David had a faithful old watchdog, and Joab thought he would settle this thing out of court; he got him in a corner and treacherously murdered him. Then David, shining high with nobility of character, refused to be dragged into the miserable affair, saying, "Your sins are too great for me. I do not approve of what you have done. Know ye not that there is a prince and a great man fallen this day in Israel?"

That is the gist of the story, but the heart of it and the point I am making is that all the while Abner had put Ishbosheth on the throne and all the while he was keeping him there, Abner knew in his heart he was not God's man; from the confession of his own lips Abner knew all the time that David was God's choice. Let us be very clear about this, for this is the central point of the whole matter. He knew God had sworn to put David upon the throne, but knowing God's will, he deliberately opposed.

I want you to notice two things, and the first is this: that although a man may set himself to fight God, God always wins. Abner tried to fight against the Almighty; he said, "I know you want David, but I will put Ishbosheth there." But God won. If you have a battle on with the Almighty, let me tell you that God will win and not you. We need never think we can lift our puny minds against the Lord of Hosts. I am glad that God has said He will set His kingdom upon His holy hill of Zion, and however the world may rage and the kings take counsel together, I know God is marching on to victory. Let the spirit of Antichrist appear, as it truly is appearing, yet God has declared that His King shall reign and He will turn and overturn until he comes whose right it is to reign.

Now coming back to our story, I want you to notice two things. Although it is true that you cannot legitimately frustrate God's plan, yet there are two things that will happen if you know God's will and oppose it. The first is that you will bring a great deal of unnecessary suffering into other people's lives. Have you ever thought of that? For two years Abner plunged the whole nation into civil war and only God knows the suffering and agony of such war. Just think of a whole country being plunged into the tragedies of civil war because one man knew God's will but would not walk in it! I want to tell you that while you fear not the trouble you may bring into your own life, if you are not doing God's will you are bringing a lot of unnecessary trouble into other people's lives. Oh, the wives whose hearts are broken because husbands will not line up with what they know is God's will for them! Oh, the parents whose hearts are heavy because their children know God's will but are refusing to obey it! Oh, the trouble that comes everywhere when men and women know God's will and do not do it! Remember, I am not speaking about those who do not know God's will; they are not in this picture.

Abner knew God's will and sinned against light. He knew, as clear as a bell, what God's will was, but he deliberately set himself against it. May God save us from sinning against light. Oh, the trouble that comes when we get out of God's will and what trouble we bring to others! May I drop a word from the standpoint of a minister as to what trouble we often suffer in the Christian ministry because of brethren who get out of God's will! The result is the same as comes from throwing a monkey wrench into the machinery. Oh, the trouble that comes on the mission field, on the evangelistic field, and in the assembly when those of us in the work of the Lord get out of God's will! I do trust that however willful I may be, by His infinite grace I shall be always kept in the center of His will.

We have given the first aspect, but the second is personal. Abner not only made trouble for countless numbers, but he himself lost all the glory of the kingdom. Oh, the tragedy of it! Just when David was coming to the throne and when the most glorious day of all history in connection with Israel was beginning to dawn, and when Abner might have shared in it, he missed it all. He was cruelly murdered and was never privileged to see the dawning of it. That is a solemn alternative for the man or the woman who knows God's will and refuses to accept it. He will never share in the glories of the kingdom, never know anything of the joy, the happiness and the blessing when the Lord reigns. I want to be there to share in the triumphs. I want to be there to share in the trump. I want to see Him and look upon His face. I want to join in the choir and sing, "Who is the King of glory!" I want to be able to travel around the world when you do not need passports and visas. And far beyond all that, I want to share in the glories of my eternal home. It is hardly necessary for me to press the obligation much farther. You can see it for yourself, and remember that Abner's story may be reproduced in your case. It is being repeated all too often. Somebody is making trouble for everyone around him because that one person is not doing what God wants him to do. Somebody is bringing sorrow because he is resisting the call of God and refusing to walk in the light, trifling with his own possibility of receiving a crown of glory that fadeth not away.

Let us make an examination of Abner's heart. I wonder what it was that made such a fine man do such a shortsighted thing. I often marvel at the shortsighted things fine people do. I often marvel at the stupidity of splendid folk. In dealing with the unsaved I have often said, "Why is it that you are not a Christian? I cannot understand it." And then there are fine Christians whom I have looked in the face and asked, "Why do you not seek the baptism in the Holy Spirit?" They mystify me. And of others I often wonder why they do not do certain things that God wants them to do. Our hearts are very peculiar, are they not? I want to examine the story of Abner and see if we can find some of the reasons that made him play traitor to his own conscience. That is the greatest tragedy of all, that he was a traitor to himself. Without repentance, there is no hope for such a man.

What made Abner oppose God's will when he knew it so well? The first thing I shall suggest is his purely *natural* love. Abner was a cousin to Saul. There is an old proverb that says, "Blood is thicker than water," and since Abner was a relative, I have an idea that one of the causes was purely natural love. He doubtless said, "Well Saul is a relative of mine and Ishbosheth is also and why should he not be on the throne?" But natural love can often lead us very far astray. You will remember the Lord Jesus said that if any man would come after Him he must put Jesus before husband or wife, before father or mother, brother or sister, or children, or houses and lands. Oh, the danger there is in being swayed by natural love! We often find when deal-

ing with young people that this is one of their chief
problems. Young people love to go in crowds, and
usually there is a ringleader, and the others do whatever
the leader does; get the ringleader and you get them all.
But I pray that our Pentecostal young people may have
better material in them than that, and have the determination to follow God's call regardless of what their
friends do or fail to do.

May the Lord save us from the snare of natural love.
It can be a very beautiful thing, but if it gets one out of
God's will, it is very dangerous. I praise God for the
spiritual friendships He has enabled me to make, and I
have always found that when we give up the natural we
get the spiritual; I have brothers and sisters all over the
world. How wonderful it is to give up for the Lord and
then get back the hundred-fold! There is really no giving up when we let God have His way; it is all rolling in.
The story is told of a man who came to Mr. Moody and
was converted. He said, "Now that I am saved, I suppose I shall have to give up the world." Mr. Moody
said, "No, you just be true to the Lord and the world
will give you up." Some people say, "If I seek the Baptism and God fills me with the Spirit, I shall have to give
up my church." But I always say, "No. No. No. Never
fear such a thing. You get the Baptism and go back to
your church. Tell them what God has done for you.
You will not have to give up the church, but something
else will happen which I need not mention." May the
Lord save us from getting out of the will of God because of our natural love.

Now the next thing I detect in Abner's heart is *natural* pride. Abner was the captain of Saul's army; he was
commander in chief. I can imagine his having a little
conversation in his own heart and saying, "You know
I am commander in chief of Saul's army; that position
in David's army is already filled, and if I get in with

David I shall have to play 'second fiddle' when I have been playing first." It is so hard to play second fiddle when you have been playing first. Natural pride got the better of Abner's heart when he said to himself, "I can be commander in chief no longer if I throw my lot with David. I shall lose my position if I go there, so I'll just keep that at all costs. I want to be next to the King." And so he said no to the will of God. I wonder how many times *natural pride* has kept God's people out of the center of His will—the refusal to take second place for a little while—what havoc it has wrought! You wanted to be at the top at any cost, and because of that you have gotten out of God's will. I travel around the world, and I do not travel with my eyes closed. I find, time and time again, that assemblies have been split by persons who, instead of being willing to fill useful places in the local assembly, wanted to be "boss" and so started other missions of their own. There was really no need of another place of worship. Perhaps some of you may be tempted to do likewise, and I hope you will remember this and refrain from falling into the snare of getting out of God's will through pride.

Some people are afraid of losing their prestige if they do the will of God. Preachers have come to me and said, "But, Brother Gee, if I become Pentecostal I shall lose my prestige." Well I should be glad to lose that to get the baptism in the Holy Spirit. Then other preachers say, "Brother Gee, if I identify myself with the Pentecostal people I shall not get any openings to preach." I know many today who are traitors to all that God has given them because they will not pay the price of the reproach of Pentecost. They are traitors to what they know is the truth, traitors to their own conscience.

Never shall I forget when the temptation came to me when I was longing to get out into the work of God and wanted meetings. An influential and wealthy man came to me and said, "Mr. Gee, I shall be happy to get you openings all over England. I believe I can use you and give you openings everywhere if you will only give up those tongues." But how could I give up tongues! As far as I am concerned I thank God that my experience in speaking in tongues is from God; it came to me when God baptized me in the Holy Spirit many years ago and after testing it out I know the experience is from God. Well, they wanted me to compromise; and when I refused, I failed in getting openings in England, but now I have them all over the world. If God has permitted anyone else to be tempted along this line, I want to say there is a tremendous field open today to those who are loyal to all the light God has given them. Oh, how we could go on talking about the danger of natural pride! I remember a friend who constantly refused to be baptized in water, and when my mother asked her the reason, she said, "Because, when they come out they look so frightful." Nothing more than *that* kept her out of the will of God. When I was in a camp meeting in Canada a preacher came up to me at the close of nearly every service; he assured me that he was hungry for the Baptism, but because he was a preacher he never would come up to seek the Lord for the experience. He is not likely to get it, and the reason is *natural pride*. May the Lord save us from this.

Then my last word as I make the examination of Abner's heart is that I believe the supreme reason why Abner refused to put David on the throne, though he knew him to be God's man, was because in his heart there was *natural resentment*. Some years before this there had been a time when Saul and Abner were chasing David and his men, and there came a never-to-be forgotten night when Saul and his army went to sleep. The sentries were posted, but they all went to sleep. David and his men were watching from the hill-top, and then David crept down notch by notch. I can see him creeping down, getting nearer, but the sentries are still asleep. Finally they get very close; David and his man get inside the line, and still their foes sleep. They creep nearer still, until at last they are right in the center of the company. One blow from David would have finished Saul, but David says, "No, I will not touch the Lord's anointed. I will let the Lord deal with him."

But David took Saul's spear and water bottle which was by his head and then left for the hilltop. They crept away until they were again safe on the hillside and then in the morning the cry rang down the mountain side, "Abner! Abner!" Abner woke up and said, "Who is that?" As he looked around he finally saw David, who called down, "Whose is this spear and whose water bottle is this? Saul, where is your water bottle?" Why Saul had had it under his pillow, but now it was gone!

And then David indulges in some sarcasm. Always be careful how you indulge in sarcasm, for there are more enemies made through sarcasm than by anything else. David said, "Arise now, thou valiant man! There is none like thee in all the host of Israel," and down in the valley Abner was writhing, for all the soldiers were hearing this. I do not wonder that the general felt bad. "Abner, art thou not a valiant man? Why do you not take better care of your master? Why Abner, someone came there and could have murdered Saul. Why I am surprised at you." I have always been a little sorry that David indulged in that sarcasm for it made an enemy of Abner, and he never forgave David for his action that night. And when the time came that he could have handed the kingdom over to David he said, "I will not do it"—*natural resentment, you see.*

Let me plead with you that you allow no natural resentiment to come between you and the will of God. Possibly someone is saying, "Yes, I would be a Christian, but I remember how unjustly I was treated by one who professes religion." And another may say, "I would come back to your church, but just think how they treated me while I was there!" Let me say that I have no excuse to offer for our mistakes; I have made them too, but I know that many of us have bitterly repented of the errors made. Our Lord said, "Go and tell your brother his faults." Perhaps if you would go to that offending brother who has wounded and hurt you, you would find that he has repented, or perhaps there was no intention of hurting you. And even if there was, it is certainly very small to allow natural resentment to keep you out of the kingdom of God. May God grant that none of us shall deliberately oppose God's will just because of any of these sins that were so fatal to Abner, and kept him out of the kingdom.

8

Can We Pray Night and Day?

"Night and day praying exceedingly." 1 Thessalonians 3:10. *"Praying without ceasing."* 1 Thessalonians 5:17. *"Supplications and prayers night and day."* 1 Timothy 5:5.

Expressions like these may well fill us with a sense of amazement and helplessness, or even incredulity, if our idea of prayer is limited to the thought of being down upon our knees pouring out our petitions in audible intercession. The wonder at Paul's words only increases when we realize that this is the testimony of an exceptionally busy man, who quite frequently combined with "the care of all the churches" personal manual labor at tent making.

How could Paul, or any other man, literally pray night and day? There are limits to physical and mental possibilities, however dominant the spiritual part of our nature may be. Sleep becomes a necessity; duties demand attention.

Two explanations present themselves. One is that Paul was only using one of those extravagant phrases in which the vehemence of his zeal delighted—"I will eat no flesh while the world standeth" (1 Corinthians 8:13)—or else that he meant it to be literally true that he *did* pray night and day and expected others to do the same. Probably both explanations have truth in them: Paul was exhorting to frequent importunate praying, but he was also indicating a spiritual activity of unceasing prayer.

We limit prayer far too much when we make it to consist only of special exercise engaged in audibly, at the expense of stopping all other activities while so engaged. That this *is* prayer in the general meaning of the word is, of course, quite understood. Such definite and unhindered literal praying should have a large part in the life of every individual child of God and in every assembly of God's people.

The cultivation and preservation of the quiet hour of unhindered pure prayer is one of the supreme necessities for all who want spiritual life maintained at a healthy level. The practice of audible prayer, even when all alone with God, is invaluable as a help towards making spiritual expression real, honest, and definite. Silent prayer may become too diffused and vague to have any meaning. At the other extreme is vain repetition of audible praying that uses merely stereotyped phrases, equally meaningless because neither the heart nor the mind is in them. The devout soul will find the middle path of sincere expressions that engage all the conscious activity of the soul, yet leave it free for a silence of real communion.

Nevertheless the "quiet hour" is vastly different from praying night and day. Is the latter literally possible? We believe that it is. And not only is it possible, but also desirable, and extremely fruitful.

We suggest that praying night and day consists of that continual prayer that can go on in the heart, and sometimes in the mind also, while engaged in the multitudinous duties that often comprise the daily round. It is a distinct possibility as much for the business man as it is for the pastor; for the busy housewife as it is for the woman of leisure. Its roots will be in prayerfulness; that is, being *full* of prayer. The heart and mind are stocked with material for prayer—often quite deliberately stocked—and then set aglow with the steady fire of faith that prayer prevails. It is something like a stove burning anthracite coal, which, when once stoked, will burn steadily for hours while constant activities go on all around it.

To achieve such prayer, problems and needs are squarely faced, and as far as possible mentally grasped, in their various aspects. They are then committed to the inner sanctuary of prayer within the heart. Once there, they are met by the sacred devotion of a heart that *believes* that God is and that He is a rewarder of them that diligently seek Him. Unless the heart is full of the spirit of prayer the mere consideration of needs or problems will be in thought only. This is purely the activity of the natural man. Thoughts need to be fused into actual prayer by the active principle of faith in the spiritual man. They must be brought to *God*.

The activity of the *mind* in such constant inward prayer must plainly be measured by and be dependent upon our necessary outward activities. Some forms of work and duty rightly demand the undivided attention of the whole conscious mind at its best; as for instance, when driving an automobile in busy traffic or when dealing with intricate bookkeeping. But at other times and in other occupations the hands may be busily employed in their appointed tasks but the mind be safely free for definite prayer in thought, or even in quiet words.

One can easily imagine Paul engaged in such prayer while busy with his tent making. Or Carey, the father of modern missions, praying constantly while working away at his boot mending, a map of the world hanging on his wall.

> "A ploughman singing at his work
> Had prayed: 'God bless them now.'"

There are thrilling possibilities in ceaseless prayer even for the busiest of people if they will cultivate true prayerfulness. In the story of Nehemiah there is a lovely little touch where he confesses that while engaged in his responsible duties as the king's cupbearer, and even while in direct conversation with his royal master, he "prayed to the God of heaven." Nehemiah 2:4. Many a Christian business man and many an active soul-winner today knows much about the same kind of dual activity.

Such inward prayer is never intended to supplant definite and active audible prayer at times and places set apart for making prayer the one and only business of the hour. The busiest of men, if really prayerful, jealously guard and cherish the prayer hour and the prayer meeting, for they know their value and necessity. Daniel prayed three times daily in a set manner (Daniel 6:10); Peter retired to the housetop (Acts 10:9); our Lord spent all night in the mountain (Luke 6:12). It is probably true that *only* those with regular habits of outward and audible prayer know the reality of inward and silent prayer as an activity distinct from merely thinking about a matter with a pious wish that God might do something.

What about the night? "I sleep, but my heart waketh." The night is often a barren time spiritually for many of us. Yet grace can so permeate the heart with prayerfulness that it overflows into the hours spent in bed. Problems and needs can be definitely placed with a real purpose of prayer upon the heart and mind before retiring, and the heart can *feel* prayer even when the mind is resting in sleep.

Possibly some such spiritual condition constitutes the background (though here we speak with considerable caution) for those dreams and visions by which the Holy Spirit has occasionally seen fit to guide the servants of God and to impart to them revelations of His will. It is necessary to remember in this respect, however, that great care must be taken in distinguishing between the purely natural results of a mind filled with either a consuming anxiety or desire and a mind and heart filled with absolutely nothing but a prayerful desire for the will of God to be done on earth as in heaven.

Praying night and day is a practical possibility for the busiest of us. Its spiritual potentialities are tremendous. The foundation for it will be laid when we diligently seek a spirit full of prayer about everything. Then taking "everything to God in prayer" will become a habit; the habit will develop into an instinct, and the instinct will make prayer a ceaseless activity pervading the whole life.

9

How to Plan Your Life

There are some who think you cannot plan and be Pentecostal at the same time. Some people have the idea that if you are really led by the Spirit your life is sort of a jigsaw puzzle, absolutely planless; that you never know what will happen next and you are liable to the most unexpected and amazing impulses that will lead you to do all sorts of things. I rejoice that it is true that we never know what may happen and that our heavenly Father does have all sorts of lovely surprises for us; yet that does not mean that we should not live a planned life.

You will note in 1 Corinthians 16:5-9 that Paul made plans. He says, "I will come," "I shall pass," "I do pass." Let us get away from some of our mistaken ideas of a life led by the Spirit, for I believe that God has a course for every life. Paul, at the end of his life said, "I have finished my course."

When I was crossing the Atlantic recently we were all interested every day in looking at the "track chart" which had marked on it a line showing the definite course of our vessel from Europe to Canada. Every day we would look to see just where we were that day and we noted that we kept to the course marked out till we came to our desired haven. So I believe God has a course for every life.

I well know that if there had been a disaster and an SOS call had come over our line, our captain would have been quite willing to answer the emergency call, and I believe we, too, as Christians, should always be glad and willing to answer any SOS call that comes to our lives, but that doesn't mean that my life is made up of SOS calls. I know where I want to go and by the grace of God I intend going there on the straightest and most direct way under the direction of the Holy Spirit.

Now the planned life should have a special appeal to those of us who are of mature, middle age, realizing that life for us is swiftly passing by and that we cannot afford to waste a single year, a single month, a single week. Life is a stewardship and not long hence we shall have to give an account of this stewardship. May the Lord help us to pack into what is left for us of life, the very most we can.

I know when you are young you feel sort of like a millionaire as far as time is concerned, and you feel you can afford to waste a few years for you are more or less immortal. I am not sure you can afford to waste such time, but at any rate when one gets to the other side of forty you will agree with me that we have come to the place where we must make the most of our time, and so I certainly believe the planned life is a good one. A planned life is so much fuller.

I am an admirer of John Wesley. His journal is my constant companion; I read it everywhere I go. You perhaps know that the movement got the name of Methodist simply because they believed so much in method. They planned their lives; they believed in being methodical in their hours of prayer, in Bible study, methodical in their ministry and when you read Wesley's life of eighty-eight years you will agree with me that he crammed into it two or three average lifetimes. I too want to get the most out of my life.

It is wonderful to be alive; it is wonderful to be filled with the Holy Spirit and wonderful to realize that if only I plan my life I can get so much into it. Looking back over the years I want to say humbly, "Thank God for the tremendous amount I have crammed in." I feel if I were to pack up and go home today I have already lived a grand life—a planned life.

Jesus taught us to live a thoughtful life. If I have one criticism to make of our precious Pentecostal folk and ministers, I think it would be that we are not thoughtful enough. Some people think that the Baptism in the Holy Ghost is a glorious labor-saving device, that when we have that we need not think any more, we need not study or meditate any more! All we need to do is to open our mouths wide and the Lord will fill them, for we are led by the Spirit; so we become lazy and then we wonder why we are unfruitful and decidedly stale. May the Lord keep us living a thoughtful life.

Jesus taught this constantly. I like His parable of the man who set out to build a tower, but did not stop to count the cost or see whether he had enough money to finish it, and by the time he had it half done he had run out of cash and could neither beg, steal, nor borrow any more; hence that tower stood as a monument to his folly. So Jesus taught us to count the cost and when we consider taking up the life of a disciple we are to sit down and think it over. I haven't any time whatever for these rushed and emotional decisions where discipleship is concerned. I am not referring to a decision on salvation for I believe that to escape from everlasting death is such a desperate thing you need to run for your life, but when we are talking about discipleship, the Lord Jesus said, "Sit down and consider. Sit down and think." Because, if you make thoughtless decisions you cannot carry out your purpose; you not only starve your own self and bring weakness into your own life, but bring dishonor upon the Name of the Lord and spread disappointment and confusion wherever you go. So may God help us to look thoughtfully at every step we take. Jesus used the figure of a king going to war against another king. If he doesn't stop to figure whether or not he has enough forces to win the battle, he may find himself in a very tight corner. That is the way Jesus taught us to regard discipleship.

Take another parable, the Ten Virgins. I believe the central application is that five were thoughtful and five were not. Five of them did a bit of thinking and figured that it was rather a risky thing to go to the marriage without having some spare oil; because they were thoughtful, they went in while the others were left out. All this teaches us the value of planning beforehand. But you say, "Did not Jesus say, 'Take no thought for the morrow'?" We must remember what that means: Take no anxious thought; don't get overburdened with anxiety and care.

Now the next thing we wish to think about is the principles that should guide us in planning our life. The first one I bring you will no doubt surprise you; the first principle you can follow in planning your life is that you can ask the Lord and then definitely plan to get your heart's desires. Some people have the idea that to be a Spirit-filled believer you must never have your heart's desire, that if you want a thing *that* is the very thing you will never have. But I rejoice that God has permitted me to have many of the desires of my heart fulfilled. And there are many more that I am planning to get. You say, "Brother Gee, we are shocked at you." But there are many things I really want and many things I want to do, and I am planning on these because I find my heavenly Father is not a hard taskmaster. He doesn't say, "Now if you want that thing, you shall not have it," but rather He says, "Rest in the Lord, wait patiently for Him and He shall give thee the desires of thine heart." Isn't that lovely! Of course I am not referring now to unsanctified, unsurrendered, unyielded desires. Because I am speaking to people who have given their hearts and lives to God and want to do God's will. I am speaking of pure desires, holy things, and as for me, I am going right in for them. I am not simply waiting for God to drop them into my lap, but I am actually planning to get them. It is lovely to walk with the Lord and enjoy this sweet, pure and delightful life in the Spirit, and let me remind you that we can bring the desires of our hearts to God.

The next principle I believe we may follow is to have a wide-open eye for open doors, for opportunities. What a wonderful thing opportunity is! The Apostle said, "I will tarry at Ephesus until Pentecost. For a great door and effectual is open unto me, and there are many adversaries." I think it is wonderful when God puts an opportunity before us, but beware of a constant love of change and a spirit of restlessness. Many a person gets out of the will of the Lord through a mere sense of restlessness, and many an assembly has made the same mistake. How easy it is simply to be guided by a desire for variety and change. One of the finest evangelists I ever knew, with such an anointing on his ministry that multitudes were saved and one assembly after another was opened as a result, simply walked right out of the blessing and from under the anointing, and to this very day is away on the shelf, out of action. And it all happened because of a mere natural love of change. It got hold of him and he had a sudden desire to travel, and he did travel and nothing has ever happened since.

I was praying in the early hours this morning and saying to God, "Isn't it wonderful that today I have the privilege of preaching Thy Word three times? What an opportunity! What a privilege!" It overwhelms me and yet I find some people throwing these privileges away. If you traveled widely in Europe as I have done, you would realize what it means to lose opportunities and to find doors closed tightly so that you cannot minister. I never appreciated liberty as I do today because I have been in places where liberty is lost. American people do not realize their privileges. You never can realize some things till you have lost them, but may God help you to make the most of your magnificent opportunities. Plan to use every chance God puts in your way.

Another thing we need to take into consideration in planning our life is not to forget the path of duty. You will notice how Paul is making his plans largely because he is taking an offering to the saints in Jerusalem, and he is planning for someone to go with him; but all the time there is that high sense of duty, a high sense of loyalty to that which means integrity of character in everything. And I want to say that I think there has not been half enough realization in our midst, where the Spirit-filled life is concerned, of the claims of sheer duty. I am staggered and indignant when I hear men and women who insult the Holy Spirit by saying that He has led them to neglect the ordinary decent duties of life. God does not do things that way. I meet husbands who dare to say that the Holy Spirit has led them to neglect their precious wives, and I meet children who think God has led them to neglect their duties to their parents. I find citizens who think that God has led them to neglect their proper duties in obeying the laws of their country. I am amazed at the way we put duty on a low level but believe that the Spirit-filled man or woman, following the path of duty, is nearly always in the will of God. It gives one a solid satisfaction to walk in the path of duty. Every assembly is blessed when it has those who are doing their job from a sense of duty. What a fine thing it is to be able to depend on the one who has been asked to be there early to open doors, to know you can depend on him 100 percent. You ask someone to sing in the choir, someone to teach a Sunday school class or anything in the work of the Lord and there are some who say, "If the Lord shows me," or perhaps they promise and then they break their promise and say the Lord told them otherwise. But my Bible says, *"Let your yea be yea, and your nay, nay."* I like people who put themselves out to keep their word, people who are prepared to suffer financially in order to keep their word. Oh, the grief we often suffer when preachers fail to keep their appointments! My duty is a sacred one and when I am making my plans I always want to have one eye on that which is my straightforward, simple duty, and plan accordingly.

Then we should be guided by our love for others. You will notice that in 1 Corinthians 16:12 Paul says, "As touching our brother Apollos, I greatly desired him to come unto you with the brethren: but his will was not at all to come at this time; but he will come when he shall have convenient time." Now of course the lovely background is that Paul and Apollos were rivals for the affections of the people at Corinth. You know the multitude is very strange; they always have their ideals and some said, "I am of Apollos," and others, "I am of Paul," and still others, "I am of Cephas." And then there are those ultra-spiritual people, little jugs of cream, who say, "I am of Christ," and many times they are the most difficult. One finds these groups everywhere. I was amused to see them in a camp meeting I once attended. There were three preachers and the people were quite divided; each group wanted to hear their favorite preacher. But the lovely thing was that God had sent three ministers with such a rich ministry that each one complemented the other and it was good for us to have some of each. Now the wonderful thing was that Paul and Apollos were loyal to one another and refused to be dragged into the personal feelings of the people. And although Paul knew that Apollos was his rival at Corinth, he said, "Apollos, you go to Corinth. You have a lovely ministry and you will be a blessing." But if Paul saw a priest of Israel in Apollos, Apollos saw another priest in Paul and he said, "No, Paul, I am not going." Some ministers I know would have moved heaven and earth to keep Apollos away from Corinth and others would have quickly seized the chance of going, but Apollos said, "No." How lovely it is when we are guided by love and respect for one another, and have the spirit of cooperation and not competition!

Now I have laid down the principles that should govern the making of our plans. But let me finish with something that is important and rather comforting, and I shall give it in the words of that great sentence at the end of verse seven—"If the Lord permit." Yes, I am sure it is quite right to make plans, but as we make them we must always write over them in great big letters of flame, "*If the Lord permit.*" Have you done that with your plans? You may make all the plans you like if you write over them, "If the Lord permit." It is more important than it may seem at first because if you say that and really mean it, it reveals the attitude of your heart towards God, which is a very important thing. It will reveal whether or not you have made the Lord the lord of your heart. Some Christians are delighted to get all they can out of salvation but they haven't given the Lord the throne. I had a coronation in my life, a wonderful coronation, when I crowned the Lord Jesus, lord of my life, and ever since I have done that, life has been sweet and wonderfully rich and full, and I am enjoying it every day. On the other hand, my mind goes back to the church in which I was saved and grew up as a boy. I remember very well, all through these years, a hard young man—a church member, but even in those days I wondered if he was saved and I am certain now that he was not. I remember the old debates they used to have in the literary society and how one of the favorite quotations of the young man was that poem—

> "I am the master of my fate,
> I am the captain of my soul."

I used to think that was a fine poem, that it displayed real power, but I am glad to say that I have surrendered my will and my life to another and Jesus is the Captain and the Master of *my* life. I was shocked and yet not altogether surprised, when just a few months back, while talking to an old friend I learned that that very fellow was serving a term in prison for a serious embezzlement. I was not surprised. He has been the master of his fate and the captain of his soul and he landed himself in prison. I might have been the same but I am glad that the Lord has been my Captain and so far He has kept me out of prison.

Now of course we must remember that sometimes the Lord's wisdom is higher than ours; indeed it always is and we must never lose that precious thing—humility of mind, realizing that we are making plans and bringing to Him a lifetime of gathered experiences. We always want to remember that God's ways are higher than ours, His thoughts higher than our thoughts and that His wisdom is greater and He always knows best.

Before closing this chapter I want to say a word of comfort to you and to myself. Our very best plans may fail and sometimes they do. I have had plans that have gone all wrong. I wonder what happens when our plans go wrong and we had written over them, "If the Lord will." What do we do about it? I know what we ought to do; we ought to take refuge in Romans 8:28 and realize that if our plans have failed He has something much better in store for us.

I want you to think of three of Paul's experiences. First of all he was shipwrecked on the Island of Melita. That shipwreck was certainly not of Paul's planning; that was never on his program. He had not expected it and had not planned for it, but it *happened* and it was a real shipwreck; and they got to shore only by swimming or on broken pieces of the ship. But read the story and tell me whether God was not making all things work together for good. Those barbarians on the Island of Melita had three months of Paul's apostolic ministry. Do you imagine that *they* had any doubts whether or not it was God's will for that shipwreck to take place? And I believe Paul had no doubt about it either when he left Melita after the shipwreck. If you have a shipwreck in your life and will yet keep sweet in God, you will thank God for the shipwreck, for He is letting all things work together for good.

There was another time when Paul's plans were changed, when he broke down with some infirmity of flesh. He had plans all made but God wanted to get the gospel to the Galatians and seemingly could not stop him in any other way so He allowed him to get down with an infirmity of the flesh.

Now I know some radical believers in divine healing wish some of these things were not in the Bible, but they are there just the same, and the only way God has been able to put the brakes on some people when He wanted them to stop was to let them get some infirmity of the flesh that made them stop in their tracks. That is what God did with Paul. Possibly he was a bit perplexed about it and disappointed, but those Galatians were praising the Lord because Paul had been stopped through his infirmity and thus preached the gospel to them; and he said afterwards, "I bear you witness, that, if it had been possible, ye would have plucked out your own eyes, and have given them to me."

Then of course there is that other mysterious passage in Acts 16 where Paul tried to preach the gospel in Bithynia but the Spirit suffered him not. His plans are all being stopped by God and at last the little party of four perplexed missionaries came down to Troas, and that night a vision came of a man of Macedonia, saying, "Come over into Macedonia and help us!" All of Paul's plans had gone wrong, but God had a better one and because of that the gospel came to Europe; and because it came to Europe it came to America and so perhaps we are all enjoying fellowship because Paul's plans went wrong and God had something better.

It may be that sometimes you feel miserable and sad because your plans have failed and you cannot understand it. May I again remind you of that glorious, victorious verse, "All things work together for good to them that love the Lord." I am certain that when we get over yonder one of the greatest joys will be to see God's hand just as much in the disappointments as when we had the desires of our hearts fulfilled; that His hand was just as mighty when our plans all failed as when they were successful; and when we get over there and see life's finished story we shall praise the Lord for all the way the Lord our God has led us. And meanwhile, I shall go on making plans.

PART II

Gifts for the Church

And He gave some, apostles; and some, prophets; and some, evangelists; and some, pastors and teachers; for the perfecting of the saints, for the work of the ministry, for the edifying of the body of Christ.

(Ephesians 4:11, 12)

And God hath set some in the church, first apostles, secondarily prophets, thirdly teachers, after that miracles, then gifts of healings, helps, governments, diversities of tongues.

(1 Corinthians 12:28)

Having then gifts differing according to the grace that is given to us, whether prophecy, let us prophesy according to the proportion of faith; or ministry, let us wait on our ministering; or he that teacheth, on teaching; or he that exhorteth, on exhortation; he that giveth, let him do it with simplicity; he that ruleth, with diligence; he that showeth mercy, with cheerfulness.

(Romans 12:6-8)

1

Ministry Gifts in the 20th Century

Not long ago the writer was entering a city in Western Canada for a time of ministry at a convention, and as the train crossed the broad river that flowed through, he was struck by the muddy and generally uninviting appearance of its waters. Later on in the day, when drinking a glass of water, he enquired rather apprehensively whether the water all came from the same river! He was assured that it did—but that there was no need for fear, because all the drinking water was taken from miles up the river, long before any of the pollution from the city could touch it.

This is exactly what nearly every true revival has been seeking to accomplish for the church—to get away back to where the pure living water of the Word of God is flowing for us from the hills of the New Testament before it becomes polluted by the "many inventions" of men in their systems and creeds.

When God began to pour out His Holy Spirit in the "Latter Rain" of these last days, there accompanied this outpouring a restoration of vision and some measure of experience concerning the supernatural gifts of the Spirit. (1 Corinthians 12:8-10). This meant a possibility, as never before, of a return to a standard of ministry in the church more in accord with the apostolic age. It cannot be too clearly recognized, or too emphatically stated, that those ministries which *God* sets in the church (1 Corinthians 12:28; etc.) are based, *not* on natural gift, but on spiritual gift—"not in words which man's wisdom teacheth, but which the Holy Ghost teacheth" (1 Corinthians 2:13). We believe the Pentecostal Movement will absolutely fail in obedience to the heavenly vision God placed before it, if it goes back to dependence upon purely natural gifts for the work of the ministry; never mind how deeply people may be consecrated, or how efficiently they may be educated in Bible schools or elsewhere. The holding steadily before us of the vision of the supernatural gifts of the Spirit, and their resultant ministry gifts, is of vital importance.

This consciousness that a return to methods and ideals in the work of the ministry more in accordance with the New Testament is one of the deepest needs of the Church at this hour, is certainly not limited to Pentecostal people alone. Mr. Roland Allen has done the whole church a great service by such books as *Missionary Methods: St. Paul's or Ours*. It cannot be denied that, with all our lavish expenditure of money, education, and organization, we are not progressing as we ought in the great task of world evangelization. The early church "turned the world upside down" in a generation. But they did it through spiritual gift, and not through natural gift: and also by methods very different from our own. In these studies we shall not be so concerned with methods as with ministries, but they are only two aspects of the same subject—a return to the New Testament.

To practically interpret the ideal of ministry according to New Testament principle in the 20th century must admittedly require breadth as well as depth of vision. We are living in a world that is outwardly (not so much inwardly) very different from the known world of the apostolic age, and there must needs be adjustment.

We believe, however, that the Eternal Spirit, and the Word of the Lord that endureth forever, are capable of that adjustment without any disloyalty to the spirit and principles of the New Testament.

There have been many sincere individuals, and many sincere bodies of believers, who have mistakenly, as we believe, sought to return in the narrowest possible sense to "the letter that killeth" rather than to "the spirit that giveth life" (2 Corinthians 3:6). For instance, such preachers have gone forth in lands as far removed from the old Judea as possible, by time, geography, and civilization—taking no purse, with only one suit of clothes, and under no circumstances to change their lodging! All this in literal imitation of Matthew 10:9-15. Obviously in such passages a distinction needs to be made between abiding principles and local circumstances. The writer has been traveling round the world preaching for nearly three years now, with at least two suits—but with no conviction of having disobeyed the principles of this passage in any way. What this passage *does* condemn is extravagance and love of luxury in preachers of the gospel. But that is another subject.

No; we believe that there can be a reasonable adjustment to our environment that in no wise grieves the Spirit or involves us in disloyalty to the Word of God. In some circumstances such an adjustment may mean a sufficient amount of organization to meet the official requirements of the State in which we desire to undertake Christian work; or it may be necessary and right, so that we may "provide things honest in the sight of all men" (Romans 12:17), for us to resolve ourselves into a properly constituted or incorporated body for the handling of public funds and the holding of property. Then in these cases we believe that New Testament principles are not being violated, but rather are fulfilled by such steps being taken. See Acts 6; 2 Corinthians 8; 1 Corinthians 9:19-22; etc. The glorious truth of the personal liberty of the individual worker, and of the local assembly, needs interpreting with breath as well as strength, if we are squarely going to face in a reasonable spirit the world-task before us today.

It appears to the writer that *the* great principle to stand for concerning the ministry is that it must be based upon spiritual gifts. This involves a recognition of the reality of the supernatural in Christian experience today: it will lead us to see afresh the lordship of Christ in giving such gifts and their resultant ministries (Ephesians 4:11) as He will: and it must result in producing among us again that which we seem to have been in danger of missing—an appreciation of the *variety* of the ministries which Christ ordained for His Church.

Before we turn in our next chapter to a consideration of that delightful variety, there remains one word of warning. *We must not confuse imitation with inspiration.* There have been hasty attempts, well-meant we believe, to establish a so-called "apostolic church" with all its nominally scriptural offices of "apostle," "prophet," etc., without always waiting for the Holy Spirit to bestow the actual endowment needed. We must not let ourselves be misled by mere labels of office. True ministry gifts consist not in name but in power. The gift will make the office: and until divine grace has bestowed the spiritual gift we can only wait and pray.

These studies are sent forth under the conviction that God's hour for restoring these things is now with us, and that a definite responsibility rests with ourselves as to whether we will be "willing in the day of His power." May they help in some way by His gracious blessing to clarify the vision, reveal the line of our own responsibility, and inspire to a faith that goes forward to possess.

2

The Giver and His Varied Gifts

The Exalted Giver on High

Our pivotal passage will be Ephesians 4; and the vision is first lifted to the source of all true ministry. "He gave some apostles, some prophets, some evangelists, and some pastors and teachers" (v. 11).

"*He gave.*" These ministries come fresh from the hand of the exalted and glorified Christ at the Father's right hand in heaven (v. 8). They are His own provision for the continual need of ministry in His Church until she has arrived at her appointed consummation; they reveal His continued love and thought for His own on earth, even though He has "ascended on high"; they represent His deepest wisdom in the perfection with which they fully meet her deepest needs for powerful witness without and steady spiritual growth within. The One who died, who rose again, who ascended up into heaven, is now the One who *gives*. Blessed tokens, these holy ministry gifts, of a living, loving, munificent Christ!

Much is implied right here at the outset; much that may be contrary to certain ideas concerning "entering the ministry." If "He gave," then there can be no question but that there is no divinely ordained ministry without His gift. It cannot be a mere matter of the human will to "do this" or to "be that." Ambition is legitimate if it be a seeking to apprehend that for which Christ has apprehended me, of seeking to be at my very best along my own God-given line of ministry: but if my ambition is simply a desire to achieve a position considered desirable by my own judgment, the judgment of my friends, or of my church—then it becomes sheer vanity, and even worse.

The divine sovereignty in this matter of our appointed place in the body of Christ in general, and in the work of the ministry in particular, is stated so emphatically that it leaves no question. The preparatory gifts of the Spirit are given "as *He* will" (1 Corinthians 12:11): the resultant ministries are "set" in the church by *God*" (v. 28): the men who embody them are "given" by Christ (Ephesians 4:11). It is often not sufficiently remembered that He has a title of the "*Lord* of the harvest," and nothing is clearer in the New Testament than the authoritative direction of the Spirit in all the activities of the Early Church. The evangelist Philip, the apostle Peter, the assembly at Antioch, the missionary band headed by Paul, are one and all seen to move in a very real and marked obedience to a divine guidance, which quite plainly sometimes clashes with their own ideas, but is nevertheless accepted as final. See Acts 8:29; 10:19; 13:2; 16:6 and 7, etc. Jesus Christ was Lord.

The methods by which this guidance was given are not so important as the principle that all the work of the ministry comes under the lordship of Christ in a very practical manner. The New Testament views Him as actively directing all operations from the throne. He was mightily "working with them, confirming the word with signs following" (Mark 16:20); but it was as their "Lord," and not merely as their helper or their comrade; even though the faithful servant had personal visitations from his divine Partner which brought inexpressible comfort (Acts 7:60; 18:9; 23:11, etc.). It will be of considerable importance that we study the methods of both the divine giving and the divine guiding; but for the moment it is vital to recognize the fundamental principle that both in giving ministers and in guiding their ministries—"*Jesus Christ is Lord*."

"Diversities of Operations"

One of the most charming things that meet us on the very threshold of studies on the ministry gifts of Christ is their wise variety.

It is true that the first on the list, the apostle, seems to embrace almost every type of ministry; but there are prophets, whose ministry is inspirational and appeals to the emotional elements of human nature; and then to balance these there are teachers, whose ministry is logical and appeals to the intellectual faculties. Note how finely these were balanced in the great missionary center of the early church at Antioch (Acts 13:1). Then there are evangelists whose ministry will be almost exclusively *without* the church: and pastors whose ministry will be almost exclusively *within* the church—both equally needed and honorable.

This matter of balance in ministry is vitally important to effective, aggressive ministry without, and well-rounded growth within; far more important than most believers realize. Many assemblies have no vision but that of a one-man ministry, which is expected to fulfill every requirement—evangelistic, pastoral, teaching, prophetic. One man is expected to have marked success in evangelism, be a splendid organizer, a good pastoral visitor, a competent Bible teacher, possessing in addition gifts of healing and inspired utterance. The marvel is that so many men seem to approximate at least in some measure to these exorbitant and unscriptural demands. Usually it is at terrific strain to themselves; and it may easily result in their never reaching a first class competence in what *is* their truly God-given line of ministry.

Other assemblies and individuals do not even seem to have the desire or vision for one man to fill every needed line of ministry: they only appear to see one line of ministry, and have neither time, nor appreciation, nor encouragement for anything beyond their own line of things. For instance, some assemblies and individual believers have no vision or enthusiasm for anything but evangelism in the narrowest sense of that term, and almost ignore teaching and teachers. On the opposite hand, there are others who would, if they had their way, have so much Bible teaching that they would turn any assembly into little more than a Bible school, and completely ignore an aggressive outside testimony. Both the above types may quite likely unite in "despising prophesyings" (1 Thessalonians 5:20), and have no time nor place for the gifts of prophecy, tongues, or interpretation. Yet at the other extreme there are those who place such an undue value and importance upon these very gifts that they do not consider a preacher to be in the blessing and liberty of the Spirit at all unless his ministry is continually sprinkled with manifestations of this description; and they like every meeting of the assembly to be dominated by these features. In each and every case there is a serious lack of balance.

What is needed is an appreciation of the *varied* ministries Christ has placed in the Church, and a realization that each and all of them are essential to well-rounded activity and growth. It is no uncommon thing to hear teachers disparage evangelists by calling them "superficial" or "sensational": and then to hear evangelists stigmatize teachers as being "stodgy" and "dry." Both types may unite in calling "prophets" fanatical and extreme; and then the inspirational folk retaliate by calling the equally God-given ministry of their brethren "carnal" and "fleshly" when, rightly understood, it is nothing of the kind. All such attitudes are wrong.

It is perfectly true that there can be extremes in evangelism which *are* superficial: there can be extremes in teaching which *are* heavy and barren: there can be extremes in prophesying which *are* most undeniably fanatical. Yet the true remedy is not to be found in repressing therefore any particular one of these lines of diverse ministry, for thereby we may all too easily quench the Spirit of God also. Indeed this has been actually done too often; men have dealt with the false and unprofitable at the terrible expense of cutting out the real at the same time. It needs an inspired touch to regulate inspired ministry. The divine plan is for each and every ministry which God has set in the church to correct and complement the other, thereby providing just the elements lacking and just the check needed to restore overbalanced tendencies on any one line—the prophet to inspire the teacher, the teacher to steady the prophet; the evangelist to continually remind us of the needy world outside dying for the gospel, the pastor to show us that souls still need much caring for even after they have been "won." The apostle above all to inspire and lead the way to fresh conquests for Christ and His Church.

We all need each other; and happy is the assembly that possesses something at least of all these varied ministries within its borders. If this seems impossible, then only less to be congratulated is the assembly or individual believer who at least possesses the scriptural vision to see that these things ought so to be, and is therefore earnestly striving to attain to it. The Lord will assuredly work for such, and delight to give His manifold gifts unto them.

The Ultimate Aim of All Ministry

The more clearly the ultimate aim of *all* true ministry in the Spirit is grasped, the more we shall appreciate the riches of divine grace and wisdom revealed in its varied forms; for the final purpose of God with regard to our salvation is so stupendous that no one line or gift is sufficient to achieve that end of itself. Paul immediately follows his list of ministry gifts in Ephesians 4:11 by stating their object: "Till we all come in the unity of the faith, and of the knowledge of the Son of God, unto a perfect man, unto the measure of the stature of the fullness of Christ" (vv. 12-16).

Note particularly this is positive and not merely negative. So many view salvation as an escape from final retribution, principally contained in the pardon of sins. The divine forgiveness is absolutely a first essential for that life of fellowship with God which is the whole secret of growth in the spiritual life; and God delights to graciously bestow this upon faith in the atoning work of His dear Son. But to view this as the sum total of salvation is like imagining that the journeys of the children of Israel were over the night they passed through the Red Sea. A modern illustration would be to think that you knew all about America directly you set foot upon an Atlantic liner at Liverpool en route for America!

Man was made in the image of God, but sin has marred that image until often it is almost beyond recognition. Yet the glorious consummation of redemption is more than once stated to be nothing less than a complete restoration to be "like Him" (Ephesians 4:13; Romans 8:29; 1 John 3:2, etc). The "measure of the stature of the fullness of Christ" is the declared goal.

Among the divinely ordained means to achieve that glorious end are these varying ministry gifts placed within the Church by the Author and Finisher of her salvation: "For the perfecting of the saints, for the work of the ministry, for the edifying of the body of Christ." It is by means of these gifts that her necessary spiritual nourishment is given, and her necessary spiritual activity carried on. It therefore logically follows that if any of these ministries are lacking from the Church there must inevitably be somewhere or other loss and hindrance to normal spiritual health and growth. If any of the gifts are developed in unbalanced proportion, then spiritual growth and activity will also become equally unbalanced, and—when viewed from the highest standpoint —abnormal. For these gifts, be it remembered, do not represent the wisdom of man in most conveniently meeting the needs he is personally conscious of; but they represent the wisdom of God in Christ providing for our deepest need from the standpoint of the throne.

The inspired illustration is the human body (1 Corinthians 12:14-28). It is common knowledge that we need varied diet for perfect physical health and strength, and exercise of every faculty is needed for all-round development. Few attain this in the natural; the brain is highly developed at the expense of the body, or vice versa. *Some* mental or *some* physical powers are perfected and hardened by continual use, while others remain dormant and flabby. In the realm of things seen and temporal this may be immaterial; but in the realm of the unseen and eternal the consequences are much more grave. The Church needs all-round spiritual growth and activity to arrive at her destined perfection in Christ. The means to this end are the ministry gifts of Christ.

3

The Apostle

Possibly the most august statement regarding apostleship is that the office has been filled by Christ Himself. (Hebrews 3:1). Of this we shall have more to say in a later study; but He ever remains the greatest example of a "sent one" (Greek, *apostolos*—a messenger, or "one who is sent"). We have His own statement, "As my Father hath *sent* me, even so *send* I you" (John 20:21). The true apostle is always one with a commission, not one who goes merely, but one who is *sent*.

Moreover, the great importance of the work involved in true apostleship means far more than being "the Lord's messenger-boy": it is an office clothed with dignity and power, always first on the list of God-given ministers (1 Corinthians 12:28; Ephesians 4:11). The apostle is sent by Christ in the same way that He was sent by the Father; and with at least something of all that implies of authority and power, and of grace and love.

The "Signs of an Apostle"

(a) These are stated by Paul, in 2 Corinthians 12:12, to have been wrought by him among the Corinthians "in all patience, in signs, and wonders, and mighty deeds." First, outstanding *fruit* of the Spirit, then outstanding *gifts* of the Spirit. The balance between the two is consistent with the New Testament all through; and probably the lack of balance between fruit and gifts is one of the principal reasons why false claimants to the office sooner or later come down with a crash. The sufferings of an apostle are such as demand the fullest possible exhibition of all the fruit of the Spirit (Galatians 5:22, 23). Beauties of character need equivalent gifts, it is true, if the vessel is to fill a place of spiritual leadership; but, on the other hand, it is still more deeply true that conspicuous gifts can plunge the possessor into the depth of spiritual disaster through pride, unless they are balanced by exceptional grace and Christlikeness—usually perfected by suffering.

The "fruit of the Spirit" in the lives of the apostles is apparent to all students of their lives; and it is also an interesting fact that all the supernatural gifts of the Spirit (1 Corinthians 12:8-11) can be traced in the experience and ministry of at least Peter and Paul; possibly John also.

(b) The personal experience of an apostle must also be something very deep and real, nothing secondhand or received by mere tradition or hearsay. "Have not I seen Jesus Christ our Lord?" says Paul (1 Corinthians 9:1) in defending his apostleship. The same type of qualification was evidently expected in all other claimants to the office (Acts 1:22; 13:2). This is only to be reasonably expected in men sent by God for positions of spiritual leadership. Their testimony and teaching must come with divine authority because of the consciousness of a personal commission from the Most High. "I have received *of the Lord* that which also I delivered unto you," says the apostle concerning the Lord's Supper (1 Corinthians 11:23), even though he might have founded his teaching quite justly upon tradition. No other ground than that of a consciousness of personal commission can stand the terrific opposition and conflict the office almost necessarily arouses. In the fierce battle waged in Galatia the apostle plants his standard right there at the outset;—"An apostle, not of man, neither by man, but by Jesus Christ" (Galatians 1:7).

The Work of an Apostle

(a) Above all else, the work of the apostle was to lay the *foundation* (1 Corinthians 3:10; Ephesians 2:20) and in this sense it is divinely fitting that the names of the twelve apostles of the Lamb occur in the *foundation*s of the New Jerusalem (Revelation 21:14). In the first sense, they laid the foundation of the church as the earliest pioneers and preachers of the gospel. In the second sense, they laid the foundation by receiving through the Holy Spirit that promised completion of the divine revelation (John 16:12-15; Ephesians 3:5) now contained in the Scriptures of the New Testament, which is the basis for all Christian faith and practice.

Such a ministry practically demanded that an apostle should combine in one man almost all the other ministries within the body of Christ. Thus he shared the inspiration of the prophet; he did "the work of an evangelist"; he knew the pastoral "care of all the churches"; and had to be "apt to teach": while in attending to business matters he followed the example of the Lord by not shunning the duties of a deacon when expedient (Acts 11:30).

(b) Perhaps the distinguishing result of all this full-orbed ministry of spiritual gifts was the power to "establish churches." This seems to distinguish "apostles" from "evangelists," if we may take Acts 8 as our guide. The evangelist could lead a revival with conspicuous success and a striking display of divine power in healing and working of miracles; but he lacked the necessary gifts for consolidating the results into an abiding form. Paul and Barnabas, on the other hand, left behind them fully constituted assemblies, with elders and deacons (Acts 14:21-23; 15:41-16:5; Philippians 1:1), that continued to grow and flourish, and to become, in their turn, centers of spiritual life and power (1 Thessalonians 1:8) long after the apostles had passed on to further conquests. Among their essential gifts would evidently be that gift of "governments" (1 Corinthians 12:28) which Weymouth translates as "powers of organization." They could point to such assemblies and say, "The seal of my apostleship are ye in the Lord" (1 Corinthians 9:2).

(c) Over these churches of their own planting the apostles exercised a natural and spontaneous authority. The "apostolic authority" of the early churches was not something arbitrary and forced, but was the logical position, spontaneously given under normal circumstances to men who were acknowledged leaders, or had been spiritual "fathers" (1 Corinthians 4:15; Galatians 4:19) to those in question. To such the apostle could legitimately say, "Are not ye my work in the Lord?" (1 Corinthians 9:1). Paul makes no suggestion of such a position over the assembly in Jerusalem, but is simply treated with the deference due to an acknowledged leader honored by God. Acts 15:12; 21:18. He was always specially anxious not to "build upon another man's foundation" (Romans 15:20), or to "boast in another man's line of things ready to hand" (2 Corinthians 10:16). There was no hint of claiming the slightest authority except where there was an indisputable right to it.

Are There Apostles Today?

The last and most difficult question concerning the ministry of apostles is as to whether such may still be found or expected in the Church today.

In one sense the answer must be in the negative. There were only twelve "apostles of the Lamb" (Revelation 21:14). It is impossible for men today to have "seen Jesus Christ our Lord" in the literal sense apparently intended in the New Testament. If we admit the possibility of a spiritual vision, such as Paul had outside Damascus (Acts 9:5), and afterwards referred to in connection with his apostleship (1 Corinthians 15:8, 9), we must remember that he evidently regarded this particular experience as exceptional—he was "as one born out of due time." Moreover, there no longer remains any foundation to be laid, in the sense in which it was being finally completed by the first apostles. They had an obvious consciousness that it was being given to them to finally complete the divine revelation for this dispensation (2 Timothy 1:13; 2:2; 2 Peter 1:15; Revelation 22:18, 19): and any supposed additional revelation today, on which a man would claim the apostolic office, is rightly to be regarded with the utmost suspicion as an almost certain mark of error and deception.

In the deepest sense, the whole body of Christ, in every generation and in every place, has been "built upon the foundation of the apostles and prophets" of the New Testament; and attempts to found sects such as, for instance, the Irvingites (or "Catholic Apostolic Church") on a supposed "foundation" of "apostles" peculiar to that particular sect are profoundly mistaken, however sincere. All true members of the body of Christ, irrespective of denomination, have an equal right to claim that they are built upon the foundation of the New Testament apostles. Whatever claims may be made to the office today, they can never pretend to be of the same nature as those of the original band; and sects based on such a claim are palpably holding a foolish and potentially dangerous error.

Does the office of an apostle exist today? Some hesitate to give a dogmatic affirmative at all. Yet 1 Corinthians 12:28 tells us that God has "set" this ministry within His Church; and Ephesians 4:11-13 reaffirms that it has been given "for the building up of the body of Christ; till we all come to the unity of the faith . . . unto a perfect man." This blessed consummation has not yet been arrived at; therefore we believe there is solid ground for expecting some form of the apostolic office to remain in active operation in the body of Christ, quite apart now from any question of laying the foundation. The New Testament itself makes it clear that the office of an apostle was not strictly limited just to twelve men: Barnabas was not one of the twelve, yet he is called an "apostle" (Acts 14:14); by implication the title is also given to James, the Lord's brother, and the leader of the church at Jerusalem (Galatians 1:19). Such apostles have a real place in "building up" the body of Christ, and typify a class of ministry which could be legitimately expected in any generation.

That it will not contain all the special marks of the apostles who laid the foundation is to be admitted; but that it will approximate to their ministry on the line of possessing outstanding spiritual gifts, and a deep personal experience, resulting in power to establish churches and provide adequate spiritual leadership for the people of God is to be legitimately demanded.

Where can such men be found? Men who owe their prominence not so much to natural gifts as to the gifts of the Spirit; men who we can truly feel have been "sent" by Jesus Christ our Lord? It is not easy to find the type of man who we feel has a just claim to be considered an "apostle" in the scriptural sense. The most likely field will undoubtedly be among our missionaries, for the very nature of their work demands and calls forth at least something of the ministry of an apostle. In a more limited sense we might sometimes see glimpses of it in the evangelistic field in the homeland; and we shall not ignore those outstanding figures who have risen at different periods during the Church's history, truly "sent" to her by the Lord to lead her into new revivals of spiritual life and advancement.

With diffidence we might suggest such names as Augustine, Columba, Luther, Knox, Fox, Wesley, Carey, Hudson Taylor, Judson, Muller, and others. Admittedly they may not fulfill all that which we consider justifies their recognition as "apostles," but the extent and result of their labors have been truly "apostolic"; and their contributions to "building up" the body of Christ have been very great. In closing, we are happy to believe that there are men today fulfilling in a precious measure the same type of God-given ministry. Let no one deny them the recognition which is their due because they neither call themselves, nor are called by others "apostles." Like every other ministry gift of Christ, the office consists not in name, but in power.

4

The Prophet

There is considerable haziness in the minds of many people concerning the real nature of the office and ministry of a "prophet" in the Church.

Some would have us believe that the "prophet" is simply another name for the preacher, and that all true preachers are prophets, and all their preaching is prophesying. There is an element of truth in this, but it plainly does not meet the case for the obvious reason that it completely fails to recognize the essential place in the prophesying of the New Testament of direct inspiration and immediate revelation.

Others simply think that a "prophet" has little to do but foretell the future. This also has an element of truth, but is very far indeed from the complete picture.

Others again have unfortunately distorted the office by trying to make its chief function that of guidance in church or private affairs; and their exaggeration and abuse of the office on this line has only added confusion, and prejudiced people against the truth. Here also there has been an element of truth, in that the Holy Spirit *does* guide at times through this channel, when He so pleases in sovereign grace; but it is never "to order," and the New Testament gives no such all-important place to prophets in the conduct of affairs.

It is unfortunate from one aspect that we no longer generally use the title "prophet" in describing the ministry of certain brethren, because this lack gives the impression that the office has ceased to exist in the Church today, or is limited to those who actually use the title. As a matter of fact we believe it is still present among us in considerable measure, and one would only expect a revival of an inspirational nature to produce a corresponding increase in this type of ministry.

The Ministry of Prophets Defined

A "prophet" in the New Testament sense is one who speaks "from the impulse of a sudden inspiration, from the light of a sudden revelation at the moment *(apoka-*

lupsis—1 Corinthians 14:30). "The idea of speaking
from an immediate revelation seems here to be fundamental, as relating either to future events, or the mind
of the Spirit in general" (Robinson). "Prophets" are
particularly distinguished from "teachers" (Acts 13:1;
1 Corinthians 12:28; Ephesians 4:11) in that the latter
exercise a more logical ministry in the Spirit, appealing
principally to the reasoning faculties of the hearers;
while the former appeal to the conscience more generally through the emotions. "Prophets" are distinguished
from "evangelists" in that while these may be powerful
emotional preachers, yet they do not necessarily minister from an immediate revelation at the moment.

The Prophet as a Preacher

In the Early Church the prophets undoubtedly provided a large part of the preaching ministry, and gave it
a distinctive note of divine authority and power which
must have been tremendously arresting to the hearer (1
Corinthians 14:25). In this they were worthy successors
of John the Baptist, and the great prophet-preachers of
the Old Testament.

To recognize this ministry today we have to look
among those preachers who speak very largely by inspiration as they go along. We personally know, and highly
esteem, certain brethren who have a singularly powerful
and uplifting ministry in the Spirit; and yet avowedly
hardly know what they are going to say when they step
on to the platform! Some Scripture becomes illuminated
to them, and provides a thought from which to start; or
some line of immediate need in the company present
brings divine revelation as to the word applicable.
Their utterances are usually without any attempt at
logical reasoning and sequence (sometimes they are
even hopelessly illogical), and yet they captivate the

heart by a declaration of truth which is convincing to the conscience. Often also they bring real enlightenment to the understanding, but it is usually through the intuitive rather than the logical faculties. Thank God for such ministry! It is often a powerful agent to promote revival.

Silas, who was a "prophet" (Acts 15:32) found a valuable place in apostolic missionary labors with Paul: and in evangelism this type of ministry has a powerful and legitimate sphere.

A word of warning is required lest this truly God-given gift and ministry should be confused with the lazy, slipshod habits of some preachers who waste precious hours which should be spent in preparation, and then expect the Holy Spirit to help them out by a last-minute revelation. Such often quote, "Open thy mouth wide and I will fill it," but their messages are usually not such as to bring much glory to the supposed divine giver. A true prophet *does* need preparation, as much as any preacher, but it is the preparation particularly of the heart. He has to "prophesy according to the proportion of faith" (Romans 12:6), and his faith must be kept living, strong, and enlightened by hours of communion with God.

It is the privilege of the prophet very often to interpret to the people the very emotion of the Spirit, entered into by a walk with God of the closest fellowship in which he shares the very "feelings" of God, if we may reverently so put it. So we may expect a prophet to be somewhat emotional. As a rule, this is a distinctive feature of his office. This may likely make him very sensitive to the spiritual atmosphere around him—reacting most favorably to a responsive audience. Yet perhaps it is one test of a prophet's true measure of divine function if he has the power to bring the Word home con-

vincingly to those who are unsympathetic. Such were
the great preacher-prophets of the Old Testament.

The Prophet as a Foreteller

The New Testament also indicates that there was a
ministry of prophets which we should hardly call
"preaching." It was too spontaneous, and—perhaps—
fragmentary. There were inspired utterances in the assemblies which brought "exhortation, edification, and
comfort" (Corinthians 14:3); or voiced some immediate "revelation" at the moment (vv. 6, 30). These were
probably brief, for "two or three" could speak in one
meeting (v. 29); perhaps even the whole company
(v. 24). Among those who thus exercised the prophetic
gift in this form were believers who spoke with tongues
and interpreted, for in this case the dual gift was es-
teemed as equal to prophesying (v. 5).

Then there were cases of distinct foretelling, conspicuously illustrated in the case of the prophet Agabus
(Acts 11:27-30; 21:11). The Early Church evidently
had confidence in the prophetic gift of Agabus, and
rightly so, for that which he foretold came to pass, thus
fulfilling the Old Testament test (Deuteronomy 18:22).
Even fulfilled prediction, however, is not a final proof of
a prophet's divine inspiration, if he deviates from the
commandments of God (Deuteronomy 13:1-5).

With regard to this type of prophet, it should be carefully noted that in the present dispensation there is no
suggestion of "enquiring" through such a gift, or of systematically applying to it for guidance. The prophecies
of Agabus obviously came quite spontaneously, and
without any seeking. It is evident from the New Testament that this was not the regular way by which the
Holy Spirit guided the Church, although He used it on
occasion.

The Prophet as a Foundation

During the period covered by New Testament history, the canon of Scripture such as we now possess was incomplete. In the early churches there were practically no Scriptures at first that dealt with the very truths of the New Covenant which were especially vital to them. They were even then only in process of being finally "revealed unto His holy apostles and prophets by the Spirit" (Ephesians 3:5). The ministry of prophets who spoke forth genuine revelations of divine truth from the Holy Spirit were plainly of incalculable value. The church was in a very real way being "built upon the foundation of the apostles and prophets" (Ephesians 2:20).

It is a serious error, however, to presume that this necessarily places the prophetic gift and office on an equality with the Scriptures for infallibility—as is proved by 1 Corinthians 14:29; 1 Thessalonians 5:19-21. Discernment as to the source, and the relative value of prophetic utterances was needed, and divinely given (1 Corinthians 12:10).

In the midst of all the prophetic ministry in the Early Church, much of it doubtless transient in interest, local in application, and apparently sometimes questionable in veracity, there was growing up a lasting body of "Prophecy of Scripture" (2 Peter 1:20) which is infallible and not of any private interpretation, and which came at an early date to be rightly so regarded. It was given to Paul and John, along with the other New Testament writers, to pen those matchless writings under the direct personal inspiration of the Holy Spirit which finally completed the glorious and infallible revelation of the written Word of God.

Henceforth the office of the prophet remains, not to add anything to the perfect revelation of the Scriptures, but for the building up of the body of Christ through an inspired and an inspiring ministry gift that interprets and applies those Scriptures with new light and life and power to every generation and circumstance by a fresh and immediate operation of the Holy Spirit.

5

The Evangelist

The word "evangelist" occurs only three times in the New Testament. "Philip the evangelist" (Acts 21:8); "He gave . . . some evangelists" (Ephesians 4:11); "Do the work of an evangelist" (2 Timothy 4:5). Its meaning of course is one who brings the evangel; a preacher of the gospel; literally, "a messenger of good tidings." In spite of these somewhat scanty references, Ephesians 4:11 makes it plain that "evangelists" constituted in the Early Church a distinct and well-recognized order of ministry, separate from that of apostles, prophets, pastors, or teachers.

The Gift of the Evangelist

Fortunately for us, the ministry of an evangelist needs no labored definition. The popular conception of the office has kept very close to the truth. We all know and love men who seem to have the good tidings of God's redeeming grace burning in their souls. Whenever they preach, their favorite theme is salvation in its simplest sense. At times they may choose other subjects, but it is very obvious that here they are most at home.

The whole Bible to men with this divine gift seems to contain nothing but the one message; they find it in type in all the stories of the Old Testament; it sings to them out of the Psalms, and inspires them from the prophets. They revel in the New Testament, for here they are most of all at home. Sometimes they amaze us, however, by the way they find gospel truth in parts of the Bible where we have seen nothing but pure history, or prediction, or doctrine applicable to believers only. Like Philip, their classic example, they are ready to commence at almost any portion of the Bible you please, and preach *Jesus!* (Acts 8:32-35). It is a glorious gift.

Their gift is plainly a direct endowment from the Lord. Philip had been chosen by the Church, and ordained by the apostles, as a "deacon" (Acts 6): he had been given no commission to evangelize; yet immediately he found himself in Samaria the heavenly gift within him urged to a preaching of the gospel, with glorious results. The same occurred at Azotus, and right through to Caesarea. We are sometimes asked to plead with young men to become evangelists. If the divine gift and calling is within them they will need no such plea: they will preach the gospel of necessity and spontaneously; and it is just such evangelism we need (1 Corinthians 9:16). Sometimes, perhaps, we may be rightly concerned as to whether a divine gift is being quenched, but the impulse to all genuine ministry must be divine. It can be ours to make an opening, but even when the Church fails here (as perhaps it did with Philip in Jerusalem), we are persuaded that a *real* gift from Christ will always somehow find or make its own opportunity.

Marks of True Evangelism

Philip stands before us in the inspired Word as our model evangelist, and it is fortunate that in Acts 8 we really have a wealth of material.

(a) *Supernatural Advertising.* Miracles of healing were a prominent part of his ministry. In view of this fact we are more than surprised at those who boast of such loyalty to the Scriptures, and yet violently oppose and condemn evangelists who pray with the sick today. Surely in this healing ministry they have the highest of precedents. Our Lord Himself adopted the same methods, and personally sent the seventy out with explicit instructions to do this very thing (Luke 10:9). It is plainly stated that this was the main reason why the people gave heed to what Philip *said* (Acts 8:6). God had evidently equipped him with those particular spiritual gifts needed for his ministry.

The principle also stands strikingly revealed that a display of divine power and blessing upon any ministry is the very finest form of advertising. No fleshly, worldly flourishing of trumpets can ever take its place if we want revival in the power of the Holy Spirit. There is a place for legitimate publicity, but we have seen advertising "stunts" in evangelistic work which are nauseating, and can only result in completely grieving the Spirit away. Divine power soon draws crowds.

(b) *The "Word" Essential.* The signs and wonders caused them to "take heed" (v. 6), but it is significant that soon after, and before they were baptized as professed believers, it says they "believed" Philip's *preaching* (v. 12). Miracles arrest and compel attention, but it is the preaching of the Word that converts and saves. Philip was no mere sensationalist, just satisfied with drawing the crowds. He preached solid gospel truth to them, and it was in believing this that they were really saved. That the work of grace in their hearts was real in the sight of God is proved by His immediate gift of the Holy Spirit as soon as Peter and John prayed for them (v. 17).

True evangelism must "preach the Word" as its central and essential factor, whatever place may be given to personal testimony, healing, or other legitimate features. The authoritative and loving call to repentance and faith must aim at moving the *will* of the sinner— not merely stirring the emotion, or tickling the intellect. It is the glorious secret of the message of the Cross that it *does* move the will, and in this is contained the ministry of the highest "word of wisdom" which Paul exercised with such effect when he evangelized Corinth (1 Corinthians 2).

(c) *The Individual Decision.* Conversion is an individual matter. Every new birth is something personal between a human soul and God. Perhaps this is partly the reason why, after the story of the mass conversions at Samaria, real though they were, the chapter finishes with the exquisite story of the evangelist and the Ethiopian—just one soul.

Herein undoubtedly lies the supreme gift of a real evangelist; the power to bring individual souls, whether in a crowd or not, to a personal determination. Someone has defined it as "the power to precipitate decision." A prophet may move the hearts of a whole company, a teacher may instruct them; but it is particularly the part of the evangelist to compel by div'ne grace to an immediate surrender of the individual will to Christ. Who would not covet such a gift? Who has not felt deeply stirred whenever he has seen it in exercise?

The Evangelist's Need of Others

The sending of Peter and John to establish the glorious work commenced by Philip in Samaria (Acts 8:14) is full of practical significance. How deeply this lesson needs to be learned, that the varying ministries given by Christ are all dependent on one another for achieving their finest usefulness and most abiding results.

First, we see how, with all his spiritual gifts, Philip lacked discernment. He had apparently baptized Simon (v. 13) upon a profession of belief, quite oblivious to the awful state of the man's heart in the sight of God. This is immediately perceived by Peter (v. 23). It is common to see successful evangelists clothed in the popular estimation with almost every known and unknown gift of the Spirit! But if wise they will recognize their own limitations in spite of the crowd.

Secondly, it was not given to Philip to impart the Holy Spirit; neither did he remain on in Samaria to pastor the work. He was divinely moved on (v. 26). The evangelist who gathers the crowd can rarely meet their need for teaching, so that they become established as a real "assembly of God": he seldom has the patience or the gift for plodding pastoral work. For an "apostle" this may be possible, Paul did it; but for an "evangelist," his true work ends where that of the pastor and teacher begins.

A Roving Ministry

The allotted task of the evangelist is undoubtedly to be continually on the move. Once he settles down he may do useful work of a sort; but never in any other sphere will he achieve the fruit possible while loyally pursuing his own divine calling. This probably was the spring of Paul's exhortation to Timothy to "do the work of an evangelist" (2 Timothy 4:5). Temporary necessities of the work were compelling Timothy to take the oversight of the church at Ephesus, but it was not his real calling, and Paul was anxious lest his special divine gift should become "rusty."

Such a ministry need not deprive of home and family joys. Philip was married, apparently had a settled home in Caesarea, and had at least four children conspicuously filled with the Spirit (Acts 21:8, 9). One of the subtlest temptations, however, that can probably come to a real evangelist is the natural desire to "settle down," and stifle the urge to still preach the gospel on fresh ground to perishing souls. Theirs is as costly a ministry as any, if it is to be loyally fulfilled.

Finally, evangelistic effort and fervor should mark the whole body of Christ. Woe betide the assembly, the minister, the believer, that ceases to be moved with a compassion, born of the Spirit of Christ, for souls. In the evangelist this passion reaches its consummation in the form of a dominating life ministry. This may not be the divine call for every one of us; but every true evangelist, while faithfully discharging his own high responsibility, also performs a glorious service to the body of Christ as a whole, when by his burning zeal for souls he quickens and inspires every member to a renewed effort to "preach the gospel to every creature."

6

The Pastor

Ephesians 4:11 is remarkable as containing the only reference in the New Testament to "pastors," although this is probably the most widely recognized of all offices in the Christian ministry today. It must be remembered, however, that the Greek word simply means "shepherd," and is literally so translated in several other places, most notably with reference to our Lord Himself (John 10:11; Hebrews 13:20; 1 Peter 2:25; 5:4), who might thus be legitimately considered as the greatest example of a true "pastor." A pastor is essentially, and above all other things, a *shepherd* of God's sheep.

The Necessity for Shepherds

As companies of believers began to be gathered together in recognized local churches or assemblies (1 Thessalonians 2:14), the need for certain ones to exercise a position of loving oversight and care would naturally arise. Such persons were required to be men more or less settled in the locality, and resident at least for a time in one place, and were distinguished from the apostles, and other ministers, who were called to move around continually.

It is plain that the early churches were put in charge of local "elders" (Acts 11:30; 14:23; 20:17, 28). These would simply be older men, who, by reason of their standing and experience, were obviously fitted to take a position of responsibility. But if the term "elder" had special reference to their age and standing, there was the more official title of "overseer" (or "bishop"—the word is the same in the Greek), which conveyed a meaning of definite leadership and official position (Acts 20:28; Philippians 1:1; 1 Timothy 3:1-7; Titus 1:7-9). "Ruling" was a definite part of the work of such elders; and some had a recognized ministry of the Word, (1 Timothy 5:17). They were commanded to "feed the flock" and "take the oversight" (1 Peter 5:2).

While many of them doubtless continued to follow their usual occupations and trades, yet it is evident that some were supported by the assemblies, doubtless because it was found necessary and expedient for them to give their whole time to the care of the flock. This is implied by Peter's warning that "filthy lucre" was not to be the motive for their service (1 Peter 5:2); and by Paul's reference not to muzzle the ox that treads out the corn, because the laborer is worthy of his hire (1 Timothy 5:18). The "double honor" of verse 17 also carries the sense of "reward" for labor; they labored "in the word and doctrine."

Combining all these references, it is easy to grasp the nature of the type of ministers called "pastors" in Ephesians 4:11. They were the recognized shepherds of the flock; and no company of believers can be gathered together for long without feeling the need of such a ministry. There is always the need of wise and competent oversight of the meetings of the assembly, so that all things are done "decently and in order" (1 Corinthians 14:40); so that the doctrine is kept sound and convincing (Titus 1:9); and so that the flock be preserved from wolves in the shape of false teachers (Titus 1:11; 2 Peter 2:1). There will also be the need of personal ministration to the members in times of special individual need (James 5:14) and of a loving care over all the souls for which these spiritual rulers in the Master's household (Matthew 24:45) will have to give an account (Hebrews 13:17). Above all else will be the positive work of *feeding* the flock (Acts 20:28; 1 Peter 5:2), because a flock well fed is least likely to become unhealthy spiritually or to give any trouble.

The ministry of men called to this work will always be primarily *within* the church.

The Divine Gift in a Pastor

The Scripture is very clear that true "pastors" are a genuine gift from Christ (Ephesians 4:11), and this is to be specially noted in a day when it seems to be thought that they can be manufactured by putting men through a special course of training. If the gift is there it can, and should be, developed (Romans 12:7); but no amount of personal ambition, or even good intention, can take its place. It is the Holy Spirit who makes men "overseers" (Acts 20:28); it is God who sets "governments" within the church (1 Corinthians 12:28).

The divine principle that the spiritual gifts bestowed logically and inevitably indicate and determine the ministry, operates here. Definite qualifications are to be looked for and demanded (1 Timothy 3:1-7; Titus 1:5-9), because these will be part of the indication of the divine call to office. God does not call a man to a task for which he has no suitable gifts or necessary qualifications.

This does not imply perfection in a man before he has any claim to fill the office of a pastor. The men who filled even the apostolic office were plainly compassed about by infirmities, and deeply felt the imperfection of their ministry. The church in every age and in every place has had to avail herself of the best material at divine disposal, however lacking in ideal qualifications it has often been. Saints of God who are inveterate grumblers at their pastors might well remember this. All honor is due to the magnificent army of men who have sought to fill the position of loyal pastors to the flock of God, knowing and feeling only too well the things in which they come short, but willingly doing their best.

Let it be clearly kept before us, however, that pastoral ministry, to be successful, *does* demand a real gift from God. It requires some measure of gift in conducting meetings, especially to maintain all things "in the Spirit," so that the wrong or fanatical is detected and controlled, and the good and true given every encouragement and liberty, with everything kept in a flow of blessing. It requires some measure of organizing ability (the gift of "governments"). It requires a large measure of tact and patience in dealing with the individual problems of the divers characters that make up every assembly. A transcendently important part of every true pastor's work is visitation (note Paul's "house to house"— Acts 20:20); but this also requires a real gift for mixing readily with all sorts of folk, and encouraging confidence. Then there is the ever-present possibility of having to exercise discipline in the assembly, and this especially requires great grace.

For all these things the great, deep necessity at the root of all else is a consuming *love* for God's sheep. A pastor needs to have a shepherd's *heart*. With this he is bound to succeed; without it he is bound to fail. But this is a gift from God, and is the surest sign of all that a man has been given by Christ to the Church for one of her pastors. Not every brilliant preacher or teacher is a good pastor: not every successful evangelist can become a shepherd also. There are "diversities of gifts"; it is not a case of disparaging one ministry at the expense of another; it is a case of seeing that each ministry requires its own proper gift from God. Happy are those assemblies that have faithful pastors watching over their souls, even though they lack outstanding brilliance in gifts of utterance. The Lord can supply this through others of His servants; but the finest results of evangelism are often wasted unless there are godly pastors ready and able to care for the souls newly born again.

Some Scriptural Patterns for Pastors

Foremost among men in the New Testament who apparently filled this office, we may probably place James, for at an early date he appears to have exercised a position of oversight and leadership in the church at Jerusalem (Acts 15:13; 21:18). Tradition affirms that he seldom, if ever, left the city; and that the integrity of his character was such that it caused him to be held in highest esteem, even by enemies of the church. His habits of prayer were such that he earned the title of "Camel-knees." Truly a notable and commendable "pastor!"

Another who appears to have possessed the pastoral gift was Barnabas. That he exercised such a ministry at Antioch with conspicuous success, for "much people was added to the Lord," is recorded for us in Acts 11:22-26. His exhortations to the converts to *"cleave* to the Lord" (v. 23) embody the very essence of pastoral ministry; for if the keynote of the evangelist's message is *come*, that of the pastor is *cleave*. Both are equally needed, though this is often not sufficiently recognized. Those beautiful qualities in his character which earned for him the name of "Son of consolation" (Acts 4:36), and which were revealed so finely in his attitude to Saul of Tarsus when the others treated him with suspicion (Acts 9:27), would fit him preeminently for a shepherd's task.

Paul, also, knew in a marked degree what it meant to pastor God's sheep; but in him the office was swallowed up in the still greater ministry of apostleship; and it was not the care of one assembly, but the care "of all the churches" that pressed upon his soul. Timothy shared his spiritual father's burdens, and although pastoral work was most likely not his particular calling, yet, like many another man, he sometimes had to do something to fill a need on that line (1 Timothy 1:3; 4:11-16). Then there were the "angels" of the seven churches referred to in Revelation 2 and 3. These were apparently the ministers or messengers of these assemblies, and it seems most likely that the "pastors" were intended.

But shining out above all others is the One who is definitely called the Great Shepherd of the sheep (Hebrews 13:20); and who is preeminently the pastor's supreme Pattern in all that pertains to his office. In patience, in teaching, in giving an example for the sheep to follow, the Lord Jesus is indeed the Good Shepherd.

Yet He Himself bases that title, not on any particular feature of ministry, however faithful or gifted, but on the one outstanding fact that "the good shepherd giveth his life for the sheep" (John 10:11), and in that statement He utters the greatest thing ever said about a pastor's ministry. This is the very essence of shepherding; for the good pastor has to give himself to death to self continually for the life of his sheep. The very antithesis is written concerning false shepherds; for they "feed themselves" (Ezekiel 34:2). The man who is in the office of a pastor for his own sake and advancement, whether it be for money, position, or fame, is the very negation of the deepest truth that the office stands for.

Among the most blessed gifts ever bestowed by Christ upon His Church, at any time and in any place, are men of whom the Lord can say that they are "pastors according to mine heart, which shall feed you with knowledge and understanding" (Jeremiah 3:15).

7

The Teacher

That teaching and teachers held a well-defined and important place in the New Testament churches is evidenced by the fact that they are mentioned in all three of the lists of ministries given respectively in Romans 12:6-8; 1 Corinthians 12:28; and Ephesians 4:11.

The last-named passage implies that their ministry was very often combined with that of the pastor, and the two offices do very frequently and naturally unite in one man. Elders who were called to take a pastoral oversight of the assemblies had a special command to "*feed* the flock of God" (1 Peter 5:2); and it was desirable that such men should be "apt to teach" (1 Timothy 3:2). But while it would seem expedient for all settled pastors to have at least some ability to teach, it does not necessarily follow that all teachers are also pastors. The teacher may be called to a roving ministry among the assemblies, similar to the apostle or the evangelist; and, indeed, the more conspicuous his gift as a teacher the more likely is this to be. A Scriptural case in point is Apollos, who plainly traveled continually (Acts 18:27; 1 Corinthians 16:12; Titus 3:13).

Teaching Requires a Divine Gift

This is, of course, plainly implied in the passages quoted above; he has a "gift differing according to the grace given" (Romans 12:6, 7); it is "God who hath set some in the church . . . teachers" (1 Corinthians 12:28); it is the ascended Lord who "gave some . . . teachers" (Ephesians 4:11). The man is not a teacher merely by virtue of natural ability and inclination; this may provide a background, but shining above and through all else will be a cönspicuous gift of the Spirit if he be a real gift of Christ to the Church.

The point seems to need emphasizing. A great many men today are teaching in the churches just because they have a natural gift for reducing all knowledge to a science, and have applied that gift to Christian truths. Their natural abilities on this line are highly trained in professional colleges, or are often self-developed by their sheer personal love of teaching others. Unhappily they may know nothing whatever of a baptism in the Holy Spirit, or a present manifest anointing. As a result their teaching will usually be either dry or divisive. How often the complaint is made with justice that "teachers are probably more responsible than any other class of ministers for the divisions that harass the body of Christ. Little wonder that in some quarters professed teachers are regarded with hesitation and suspicion, rather than welcomed with open arms.

All this indicates the lack somewhere of a great essential. No ministry in the power of the Holy Spirit is ever "dry"; it will convey "rivers of living water" (John 7:38) by whatever particular gift it operates, and quite as much in teaching as in evangelizing or prophesying. Paul finely described the teaching ministry of Apollos as "watering" (1 Corinthians 3:6), and such all teaching by a spiritual gift will surely prove to be. The saints will be left refreshed and revived, for it says of Apollos "he helped them *much*" (Acts 18:27).

Moreover, the only divisions caused by teaching in the power of the Spirit will be owing to definite unbelief and hardness of heart in the hearers, as in the ministries of our Lord and Paul and the apostles. There will not be unnecessary divisions caused among sincere and simple-hearted believers, as is often the case when some so-called teacher has been around among them pushing his own personal "stunts" on the doctrinal line. The true teacher will shun causing division as he shuns the plague, except where it is unavoidable over some great fundamental issue. His work is to build up the body, not to divide it.

But for such a ministry to be accomplished in real power he requires more than natural gifts, even though sanctified. He needs a special grace from God and those foremost gifts of the Spirit which are as essentially supernatural in their real character, when rightly understood, as even diversities of tongues or gifts of healing. His dependence will be utterly on the anointing of the Spirit, even though his appeal will be made to the logical faculties of his hearers, and operate through the logical and reasoning faculties of his own understanding enlightened by the Holy Ghost. The real teacher who is a gift from Christ will usually be orderly in his discourses, for that is of the very essence of his own particular ministry; quite consistently he may speak from notes and follow a carefully prepared sequence of thought; but at the heart of it all is a supernatural gift of the Spirit quite distinct from the same outward process followed by a teacher leaning only to the natural mind and limited strictly to natural resources. Those who have listened to the two different classes of ministry know the difference. The one is of the Spirit, and bringeth *life;* the other is of the letter, and killeth; even though it temporarily tickles the ears and pleases the vanity of the hearers.

The Value and Necessity of Teachers

Experience has proved that the ministry of teaching has sometimes been sadly undervalued, to the serious detriment of the work of God. The stirring campaigns conducted by God-sent apostles and evangelists, with their impressive array of converts, and air of revival, provide a tangible evidence of a spiritual life and victory which captivates the popular mind, and makes folk feel that something is really happening. The same is true of those beautiful ministries where the sick are healed, and demons cast out. Let it not be presumed that in the ministry of the teacher, however, there will be no converts made, or no sick ones healed; blessed be God, the reverse is true, for God loves to honor His own Word, in whatever form it is preached. Nevertheless, for the most part the ministry of a teacher will be less openly spectacular than that of these other brethren, and to the casual observer will provide less in the way of what he may choose to call "results." The teacher's work is not so much to evangelize, as to "help much those who *have* believed through grace" (Acts 18:27); he is usually called to "water" that which another has planted, and to "build" upon a foundation already laid by another servant of the Lord (1 Corinthians 3:6-10). Before God, the planter and waterer are of equal value and importance (verse 8). If sometimes men seem to accord a far greater appreciation to the successful evangelist, then the teacher must gladly carry his cross, and happily and faithfully discharge his ministry as unto the Lord and not unto men.

It has often been a regretable fact that results of very successful evangelistic campaigns have been largely wasted because no adequate provision was made for pastors and teachers to follow on, with their equally essential ministries. Yet how careful the apostles were to make provision on this line (Acts 8:14; 11:22; 14:21-23; 15:36); and so on. If some assemblies are in danger of stagnation through lack of evangelical zeal, it is equally true that some others are in the same peril, and perhaps in a deeper sense, through lack of teaching and soul food.

Individual believers have also erred on the line of undervaluing teachers, by misunderstanding 1 John 2:27. They hastily presume that teachers are quite unnecessary for those who have received the fullness of the Spirit. Scripture must always be balanced with Scripture, however; and it is probably sufficient answer to this that God has set "thirdly teachers" within the church (1 Corinthians 12:28, etc.). The Lord would not appoint them if there were no work for them to do! The proud spirit that scorns teachers invariably ends in a pitfall of hopeless fanaticism and miserable shipwreck. We all need humbly to learn from each other, remembering Ephesians 4:16. The real meaning of 1 John 2:27 is doubtless that believers who have received the anointing are able to discern between true and false teachers, and can receive that personal revelation from the Spirit of God regarding the truth that makes it a part of their own spiritual life in Christ. That they cannot dispense with teachers, however, and are not meant to, is proved by the fact that in this very verse John is teaching them! Indeed the whole epistle is practically all teaching.

The Temptations of Teachers

The fact that teachers so often produce confusion and division, rather than revival and blessing, calls for solemn consideration. Moreover, it is not only because men often teach who have had no divine call and possess no real spiritual gift, for sometimes it has been regretably true of men conspicuously baptized in the Holy Spirit and genuinely gifted for such a ministry.

In the possession of spiritual knowledge, which is the essential foundation for any teaching ministry, there lies a subtle temptation to pride (1 Corinthians 8:1). This may be true even of knowledge received by a gracious revelation of the Spirit of God. To hold real knowledge of the Word and ways of God with the simplicity of a little child, and deep humility of mind, is a mark of true greatness in a teacher. One of the most beautiful incidents in the Earth Church is where Apollos, gifted, eloquent, and "mighty in the Scriptures," is spoken of as being willing to sit at the feet of two humble tentmakers while they expound "unto him the way of God more perfectly" (Acts 18:24-26). No wonder God could, and did, give to this man a ministry of singular power and helpfulness to the saints!

When a teacher ceases to be teachable himself, when he refuses to give due weight to the light and experience vouchsafed to others also, when he is unwilling for his doctrines to be submitted for the approval of the whole body, then he becomes positively dangerous. Almost invariably he will become either a heretic or a schismatic.

Paul beautifully describes the true attitude towards all our "knowledge" for the present, when he points out that even though it arises from the possession of a spiritual gift quite as supernatural as tongues or prophecy, yet it is still true that we only "know in part," even as we only "prophesy in part" (1 Corinthians 13:9). This should sufficiently check a dogmatic spirit in either a teacher or a prophet. We know nothing yet in that perfection and balanced accuracy that we shall possess when we "know even as we also are known" (v. 12), even though granted spiritual gifts. Moreover, other brethren may have had rays of light granted to them along certain lines of truth which have been up till now withheld from us, and vice versa. For the whole truth that we can build the body up in divine love, we need that which "every joint supplieth." In the fusion of some apparently conflicting lines of thought and teaching there undoubtedly lies many of our richest discoveries of the divine wisdom and grace.

The emphatic and unwavering declaration of those things most surely believed among us, coupled with a humbleness of mind always ready and open to receive fresh glimpses of truth, surely marks a teacher who, in receiving a gift, has also not come behind in receiving the grace of our Lord Jesus Christ.

8

Some Other Ministries

Ephesians 4:11 is apparently intended to be a representative list of ministry gifts, rather than an exhaustive one. There are two other catalogues of such ministries given in the New Testament (Romans 12:6-8; and 1 Corinthians 12:28), both of which contain added items, and a slightly different definition of the same offices. Taken together, the three passages reveal the extraordinary richness and variety of ministry with which the Early Church was endowed; and stir our hearts with a longing desire that the Church today might equally come up to the divine standard and enjoy these rich provisions of His grace.

Taking Romans 12:6-8 first: we immediately recognize prophets and teachers; while "rulers" may probably be synonymous with "pastors" of Ephesians 4:11

(see chapter 6). But in addition we find "ministers" (Greek *diakonos*), "exhorters," "givers," and "those who shew mercy."

Turning to 1 Corinthians 12:28, we again find apostles, prophets, and teachers; while "governments" is probably the equivalent of "pastors" and "rulers" in the other lists. "Miracles" and "gifts of healing" are here regarded as distinct ministries, but we have already seen that these gifts had a special place in the ministry of evangelists, though not confined by any means to that office alone. "Diversities of tongues" is also regarded here as a definite ministry set by God in the Church; but judging from 1 Corinthians 14:5 this would approximate very closely the ministry of prophets when coupled with the gift of interpretation (as it always must be when exercised in the assembly, (1 Corinthians 14:5, 13, 28). It is inspired utterance, but of a more rapt and ecstatic nature. There still remains the suggestive office of "helps," and for this we find no adequate parallel in Ephesians 4:11, though we believe it is supplied in Romans 12.

It must be noticed that the divine sources of the ministry gifts of Ephesians 4:11 is equally emphasized in these other lists: "As *God* hath dealt to every man . . . gifts differing according to the grace that is given us" (Romans 12:3-6); "*God* hath set in the Church." (1 Corinthians 12:28). However lacking some of these ministries may appear to be in any supernatural element, yet all alike are described as coming from a supernatural source, given by the "same Spirit," and received through the same grace—teaching as much as prophesying, ruling as much as miracles, helps as much as diversities of tongues.

As a matter of fact, one of the most striking features of these lists is the way that ministries which we would rigidly divide into "natural" and "supernatural" are all jumbled up without any sense of incongruity, so that "miracles" comes in the middle of the list. The question arises, Are any of these ministries to be regarded as purely natural in the ordinary sense of the word? Consideration of this vital point will be left for our next study: for the moment we had better confine ourselves to a closer examination of some of these "other ministry gifts."

"Helps" (1 Corinthians 12:28)

This is a delightfully suggestive title for an office. The actual word used here, *antilepsis,* occurs only in this place, and the lexicon gives us as its meaning, "a helper, reliever." A term like that can embrace so much! Probably the best commentary will be found in the parallel list in Romans 12:6-8, and there we can locate "helps" among "those who shew mercy." The thought is especially ministry to the afflicted and needy. Moffatt translates verse 8, "The sick-visitor must be cheerful"; while A. S. Way renders the passage even more beautifully— "If you come with sympathy to sorrow, bring God's sunlight in your face." Such are "helps" indeed! and what a vast field of ministry within all too easy reach of every one of us it opens up. To fulfill it worthily, however, according to these inspired instructions, we require a real equipment of divine grace and power. Those who are filled with the Holy Spirit have plenty of opportunities for the outflowing of "living water" other than merely preaching, and it is good to see this in the Word.

Phebe (Romans 16:1, 2) was one of these "helps." It says she was "a succourer of many." Once again the Greek word is suggestive: it means "one standing before," a shielder, a protector. Even Paul the apostle had been shielded from suffering at some time or other by this faithful sister in the assembly at Cenchrea.

In verse 3 he touchingly refers to two others who were his *"helpers* in Christ Jesus"— Priscilla and Aquila. They had even risked their lives in shielding him.

A beautiful example of their ministry of help is also shown in Acts 18:26, where they take Apollos and "explain unto him the way of God more perfectly"—leading that already gifted teacher into the full blessings of Pentecost. Then Apollos went on his way with new power to "help" others (v. 27).

Also there was "Mary, who bestowed much labor on us" (Romans 16:6): and "Gaius mine host" (verse 23 and 3 John); with a host of others whose names are scattered up and down those intensely human documents which make up the inspired Scriptures of the New Testament—men and women who were "helps" in a very literal sense. Some there were who excelled in hospitality: others opened the doors of their house to the whole assembly, like Aquila and Priscilla (1 Corinthians 16:19), Nymphas (Colossians 4:15), and Philemon (Philemon 2). These were probably among the more wealthy members, and lead us to consider

"Givers" (Romans 12:8)

We do not sufficiently regard giving as a real ministry, entrusted to us by the Lord. We fear there are still those who regard it as a somewhat burdensome necessity of the work, at the best nothing more than a duty not to be shirked. Thank God for those who view it as a privilege. Yet properly understood from the Scriptures it is far more than all this; for, to be rightly engaged in, it will become a fine art, and will manifest a divine gift. Happily we may all share something of this grace, but its special expression will be for those entrusted either by divine providence with personal wealth, or by the Church with administration of her united resources.

A. S. Way helps us here again; "He who has wealth to distribute must do it without affectation," is his illuminating paraphrase of "He that giveth, let him do it with simplicity." Consistently with the principle here enforced, Paul includes "bestowing all my goods to feed the poor" (1 Corinthians 13:3) in his tremendous teaching that all spiritual gifts are valueless unless exercised in an atmosphere of love.

Giving, in the Early Church, was as much a recognized ministry as teaching or healing, and required to be equally fulfilled in the power and grace of the Spirit. Those who had wealth entrusted to them were stewards of a God-given means of ministry which was to be used in the whole body quite as much as the ministry of prophets or pastors—not to dominate the body because of their wealth, but to fit in as an integral part of the whole. Or if they were officially appointed administrators by the church, to discharge their office in a way to bring blessing to all. We need to catch again the early vision.

"Ministers" (Romans 12:7)

"Or ministry, let us wait on our ministering." The term "minister," *diakonos,* is often used broadly in the New Testament for all who ministered in holy things, including the apostles themselves (e. g., 1 Corinthians 3:5; Ephesians 3:7); but in this case it evidently has a distinctive sense from the other ministries mentioned, and approaches more closely to the type of ministry literally called "deacons" in Philippians 1:1; and 1 Timothy 3. The same word is used of Phebe in Romans 16:1, where it says she was a "servant" (literally, *diakonos*) of the church at Cenchrea. This office in the

Early Church was especially connected with having charge of the alms and money of the assemblies, and being an overseer of the poor and the sick. We do not always associate this class of ministry with any special divine gift, but perhaps it is as well to catch the added dignity which such a passage as Romans 12 places upon it. We are then in a better position to understand the high qualifications demanded in 1 Timothy 3. Something more than merely natural business ability is required, and the grace of Christ is manifested as readily in "serving tables" aright (Acts 6:1-5), as in preaching. This also is a real gift from the Head of the church, and assemblies looking for "deacons" might well remember this.

"Exhorters." (Romans 12:8)

This is the only place where exhortation is mentioned as a separate and distinct ministry. Usually it is regarded as a natural and essential part of almost every other ministry, the primary thought of course being encouragement, either on the line of comfort or of stirring up. With some, however, it was evidently a special gift for the ministry—Barnabas being a case in point (Acts 4:36). In such cases, where a special power on this line was recognized, the one so gifted had to specially cultivate and diligently use it, even though exercised in conjunction with other definitely recognized offices.

There is no necessity to regard any of the offices of the Early Church as representing a hard-and-fast line of limitation to one particular form of ministry. Doubtless they often mingled and blended as occasion demanded in one servant of the Lord. Nevertheless each one would have some special line of ministry in which the power and grace of the Spirit would more conspicuously flow in liberty and fruitfulness, so that it would come to

be regarded as their distinctive office. The principal
teaching of these three passages is that the Church has
been divinely endowed with a wonderful variety of ministry gifts, sufficient to meet her every need. Arising
from this comes the personal responsibility of the individual to exercise his own particular gift at its very max-
imum of usefulness, through a love which is divine in its
origin, but exceedingly practical in its application.

9

How Ministry Gifts
Are "Set" in the Church

Having now considered the various ministry gifts in
detail, we turn to the practical question of how they are
"given" by the ascended Christ, and thus divinely "set"
in the Church.

It will be as well first of all to examine two opposite
theories, representing two extremes of opinion, before
seeking the balanced truth between the two.

Are They Natural Gifts Sanctified?

This is the usual line of thought; and it has this in its
favor—that it rightly gives God the glory for every
purely natural ability we possess, and it recognizes that
the supreme and proper attitude to adopt with every
such gift is that of its entire consecration to God and
His service. This is very true, and it opens up a large
and delightful field of opportunity for varied ministries

from us all. There is scarcely a single thing we are capable of doing, from cooking and carpentering, to singing and writing, which the Lord cannot make use of if laid at His feet. Moreover, the anointing of the Spirit resting upon the individual will bring a true unction upon the most natural ability.

Yet, while all this is delightfully true, we cannot but recognize that the New Testament implies something beyond natural gifts, however useful and sanctified, in the ministry gifts with which Christ has enriched His Church. For two reasons at least—

(a) These ministries are a direct result of an operation of the Holy Spirit (1 Corinthians 12:4-7); they arise from the grace of Christ in the believer (Romans 12:4-6); and are the definite gifts of that grace to the body (Ephesians 4:7-16). But purely natural gifts are possessed by saved and unsaved alike. Men and women who are unregenerate and can know nothing of the indwelling Spirit (John 14:17) may possess identical natural gifts with the believer. In this case the only difference would arise through their consecration by the child of God to divine service. But the emphasis in the Scripture is upon a special divine bestowal, not upon an act of human consecration. Where consecration is urged it is based upon our duty with regard to gifts already given to us by divine grace because we are believers (Romans 12). Our consecration does not bring a supernatural element into what was before a purely natural gift; it may bring a supernatural blessing upon it, but that is very different.

(b) Some of the gifts mentioned in the New Testament are undeniably supernatural; e. g., gifts of healing, miracles, and tongues. Yet the Scriptures never give the slightest hint of a classification of the ministry gifts into "natural" and "supernatural." So striking is this that even Conybeare and Howson are constrained to state,

"These miraculous powers are not even mentioned by the apostolic writers as a class apart (as we should now consider them), but are joined in the same classification with other gifts, which we are wont to term natural endowments or 'talents'" (*Life and Epistles of St. Paul,* chapter 13). But is it right now to consider them "as a class apart"? Are we Scriptural in being wont to term them "natural endowments"? Such a distinction is quite unscriptural, and for that cause likely to result in our missing vital truth. Logically, we are left with only two alternatives: one is the modernist position which drags all the supernatural down to the level of the natural, and makes "gifts of healing" become the practice of medicine, and "diversities of tongues" become a knowledge of foreign languages; the other is to revise our conception of ministry gifts which we have been wont to term "natural endowments," and to recognize that if they are indeed the ministries mentioned in the New Testament, then they are essentially supernatural.

How Can We Discern the Supernatural Element?

In the ministry of apostles and prophets this may present very little difficulty, but it will not be so obvious at first sight in the office of evangelists, pastors, or teachers. We can all see the miraculous in gifts of healing and diversities of tongues, but not so readily in "governments" or "helps." Yet our study so far has led us to expect that the supernatural element *is* there, and it is not unimportant that it should be recognized. Apart from anything else, it may save us from placing that exaggerated stress upon the more outwardly supernatural gifts which was the very error of the Corinthians, and which always tends to fanaticism and an unbalanced testimony.

The supernatural element in ministry gifts will always

be inseparably connected with the minister's anointing of the Holy Spirit, not only in public service, but upon his individual life and experience as a baptized believer. Thus the teacher, who brings to the people the spiritual gift of the "word of knowledge," has received his illumination by a distinct operation of the revealing Spirit of Truth. The purely natural abilities and characteristics of the believer may provide a background upon which the Holy Spirit works with His supernatural gift; and, indeed, this is never more clearly instanced than in the personalities used by Him for the writing of the inspired Scriptures. But the ministry gift is something added by the Holy Spirit. In the case of the teacher it will be the logical faculties which will be at work, but besides the purely natural and proper activities of the mind, there will be the added revelation and inspiration of the Spirit of God.

So also with the pastor; if he has a spiritual gift of "governments" his office will be marked by a discernment, a wisdom, a grace, which he would never have possessed in the natural, even though born with an innate tact and capability for management. And so on, right through every ministry, even to the work of "helps" and the necessary work of service in the church on purely business lines. There will be a distinguishing element from anything we can find in the world. That distinguishing element may be hard to define, but it is none the less real. It is "better felt than telt." It is easily recognizable by those who also have received the same Spirit.

Are Ministry Gifts "Set" Through Prophecy?

We now turn to the very opposite extreme from those who see only natural gifts consecrated as the divine method of setting these ministries in the Church. By a natural swing of the pendulum there are those who so emphasize the supernatural bestowment contained in a ministry gift that they insist on its being revealed by a prophetic utterance, and base upon this theory a complete system whereby all offices in the church are allotted in this way. The recognition this gives of the essentially supernatural element in true Christian ministry is refreshing; but it is unbalanced and unscriptural, and therefore full of mischievous tendencies.

In actual practice it often lamentably breaks down. Men are named for certain offices in the church by the "prophets" who have, all too obviously, none of the particular spiritual gifts and qualifications which such a ministry demands. A state of things is produced which ends in a fiasco, to the disappointment of the individual and the church, and the dragging of the testimony into reproach and ridicule. The reason for this may most usually be found in the false character of the prophetic utterances, which probably came merely from the prophet's own heart (Ezekiel 13:2, 3). But it should also be seen that this was more or less inevitable, because the prophetic gift and office in this case (even if originally genuine), have become linked up with a system which is unscriptural, and therefore cannot be used by the Spirit of Truth.

It is usual to quote Acts 13:2 for Scriptural support for this practice; but that was *not* a calling to any "office," for these two men had received a personal divine call to their lifework long before. This occasion was simply a call to a special piece of missionary work which it states was definitely completed in Acts 14:26. With more justice we might turn to 1 Timothy 4:14, for it is evident that there were some striking prophecies uttered (chapter 1:18), probably at the time of Timothy's setting apart for the work of the ministry (Acts 16:1-3). That which Timothy then received, however, was a *gift*, as is plainly stated in 2 Timothy 1:6; and if any recognized office afterwards arose from this divine bestowment, it was only because of the exercise of the gift. This leads us, finally to see that—

It Is the GIFT That Indicates the OFFICE

This Scriptural principle is so logical and fundamental in the very nature of all things in the divine economy that we marvel there should be any departure from it under any pretext. Thus we find Paul, in the early part of 1 Corinthians 12, with perfect consistency, stating the various gifts of the Spirit with which believers are endowed, and then, at the end of the chapter, naturally gliding into a statement of the resultant offices or ministries which come from them. God "sets" in the body by the bestowal of various gifts for service, and the gift given indicates the particular work to be done. There is not the slightest hint of any other indication, either by prophecy or any other method. Such a verbal indication would plainly be superfluous, for the gift itself will be self-evident. The same principle is also recognized in Romans 12 and Ephesians 4.

Every ministry gift of Christ consists *not* in a title of office, but in a fruitful ministry along a certain line. Thus even the apostle supported his claims to recognition as filling that office, *not* merely by reference to an arbitrary "call" or by a prophetic intimation or vision (though he, of all men, might have done so), but by an appeal to the "signs of an apostle" (2 Corinthians 12:12) and to the *fruit* of his labors (1 Corinthians 9:1) and so on. In the same manner the prophet could point to his predictions fulfilled, as Agabus (Acts 11:27, 28; 21:10, 11); the evangelist could point to definite converts under his preaching of the gospel, as Philip (Acts 21:8; 8:12); the pastor could point to an

assembly steadily built up and flourishing, as Barnabas
(Acts 11:24); and the teacher could point to believers
who had been mightily helped and edified, as Apollos
(Acts 18:27, 28).

The divine method by which the ministry gifts of
Christ are set within the Church thus makes the supernatural delightfully practical. The gift which every believer receives from the Holy Spirit infallibly indicates
the office to be filled. That gift needs maintaining in active exercise—but this demands a separate study.

10

Ministries We Lack;
Our Responsibility

It is a regretable fact that certain of the various ministry gifts of Christ are often found lacking in the
church; perhaps not universally, but sometimes for a
season, and often locally or even in great districts.

In the experience of the writer, he has found whole
districts where one or more of the ministry gifts have
been found lacking in a way calculated seriously to en-
danger the balanced presentation of the gospel and
growth of the church. In one case the shortage has been
in evangelists, with a corresponding loss of agressive
zeal; in another country the need has been exactly opposite—scores of consecrated evangelists but hardly
any teachers, so that converts were languishing for the
Word. In other instances great territories seemed to
lack, in the one instance pastors, and in another in-

stance prophets, the result being that in the first case very little solid work was resulting from much commendable evangelistic effort, while in the second case there was a tendency for the distinctive place of inspired utterances in the church to be despised and forgotten and ultimately to die out.

Then there are needy fields in many parts of the world still waiting for apostles in the true sense of the term—fields where the burning passion of Paul to preach where Christ had not been named, and not to build upon another man's foundation, can still find scope for actual and literal expression. Other fields there are where those with lesser gifts are faithfully toiling on, longing for one to come with a divine equipment capable of really leading the forces of the church on to victory.

Has Christ Failed to Give?

This question forces itself on the mind. Recognizing that gifts from the risen Christ constitute the Church's true ministry, implies that the lack is because the necessary gifts have not been given. In that case our responsibility would seem to be at an end.

Such a position, however, reacts in the form of an aspersion that somewhere Christ has failed—an aspersion instinctively and rightly rejected by all who know and love Him as their Leader. Moreover, such an attitude leads to that mistakenly fatalistic position into which we are always trapped when we magnify the sovereignty of God to such an extent that we forget human responsibility altogether.

The mighty Victor over the tomb is still leading the Church on to certain victory, and His ability and willingness to give all needed gifts unto men, even "for the rebellious also," compels us to look elsewhere for the

explanation of any lack we may find in our possession
of vital ministry gifts among the assemblies.

The Responsibility of the Church

We have already seen that the basis of the ministry
gifts of Christ will be found in the possession by various
individuals of spiritual gifts. Now the sovereignty of
God is very emphatically stated with regard to these
gifts—"as *He* will" (1 Corinthians 12:11), "*God* hath
set" (12:28), "*God* hath dealt to every man" (Romans
12:3), and so on.

But this does not preclude the necessity of prayer for
the gifts, nor of human responsibility in their exercise.
Thus we are told to "covet earnestly the best gifts" (1
Corinthians 12:31), and to *pray* for additional gifts to
those already possessed (1 Corinthians 14:13, 39).
Moreover, we are reminded forcefully of the necessity
of faithfully discharging our various ministries in the
body (Romans 12:6-8); and in this respect note especially Paul's strong words to Timothy (1 Timothy 4:14
and 2 Timothy 1:6).

Now this principle of the privilege and responsibility
of the individual believer to prayerfully cultivate and
diligently sustain a high condition of competency in the
exercise of spiritual gifts, in cooperation with the sovereignty of God in their bestowal, applies also to the
Church as a body. We purpose dealing with the responsibility of the individual in our next chapter; but for the
moment we are thinking in large terms of the Church as
a whole, or of assemblies and groups of assemblies
united.

There need be no hesitation in affirming that wherever and whenever assemblies of believers are lacking in
certain ministry gifts, and are alive to their lack, that
they thereby become responsible for taking every right-

ful means God has placed in their power for remedying such a condition. What are those means? To this practical consideration we now turn.

The Remedy for Lack in Gifts

(a) *Prayer.* The Early Church "continued with one accord in prayer and supplication" for Pentecost, even though the promise of the Father had been assured to them by a renewed pledge from the risen Lord (Acts 1:14, 15). The Corinthian assembly, as we have already seen, were exhorted to *pray* for spiritual gifts not fully enjoyed, even though God gave them as He willed. The Church, in like manner, should pray for whatever ministry gifts she may feel the lack of at any time, even though Christ bestows them in sovereignty. The very attitude of prayer will, in itself, place the Church in the spiritual position where Christ can most readily grant such gifts. Prayer is so obviously a first essential in the matter that further emphasis seems superfluous.

(b) *Encouragement.* This seems far more in need of stressing, at least on the line of understanding *why* we lack certain ministries.

Experience has taught us that frequently some lines of ministry are lacking in many assemblies for the simple reason that they have received practically no welcome or encouragement. For instance: assemblies which have rightly stressed aggressive evangelism, but with perhaps a rather narrow vision of what "evangelism" truly consists of, have often given scant encouragement to any of their members, young or old, whose spiritual gifts fit them the rather to be pastors or teachers. At the other extreme are assemblies who make so much of teaching "the Word" that members with a bursting desire for evangelism get little opening or help.

Other assemblies noteworthy for evangelistic activity,

and also not unmindful for the rightful place of teaching, will nevertheless systematically discourage all manifestations of prophetic utterance, or speaking with tongues—probably through fear of fanaticism, or ignorance of how to order the exercise of spiritual gifts. Then some assemblies will swing to the opposite side of the pendulum and so overestimate the importance of inspirational gifts that they do not see the Holy Spirit in the word of wisdom or the word of knowledge at all, but think that all logical ministry is purely natural, so that a man is thought nothing of unless he always speaks by sudden revelation at the moment; and "prophets" rule the situation.

The actual result in all such cases is that some of Christ's ministry gifts receive so little encouragement and such a cold reception that they never develop into real usefulness in the body nor become properly recognized. The remedy is simple: equal encouragement to each and every diverse line of ministry placed by Christ in the body, and *especial encouragement to that which is most lacking* until the balance is restored.

If it is that pastors are lacking, then young men who are conspicuous for loving patience with souls and tactful gifts of administration might well receive that pushing and encouragement more usually extended to those who promise brilliant gifts as preachers only. Where prophets are lacking, the tiniest flame of genuinely inspired utterance should be sheltered from every quenching fog of doubt and prejudice, or where teachers seem almost unknown the assemblies might well see whether those among them who can minister logically to the "understanding also" are not being snubbed as perhaps "not Pentecostal enough."

(c) *Recognition.* Finally, there is a likelihood of the various ministry gifts of Christ being more or less present, but unrecognized, at least as regards the fact that they are fulfilling the actual offices of the Scripture. While in this case the Church may not be suffering from lack of ministry, yet there may thereby be considerable unnecessary restlessness among the saints. It is good that all true ministry gifts in the Church should therefore be recognized for what they are, whether apostles, prophets, or whatever they may be. This will make for their true place being conceded to them, and tend to a smoother working all round, with less crying for what we already actually possess, but more determination to see it operating in that glorious fullness of power by the Spirit of God, which makes every ministry gift in its own sphere a mighty weapon for the pulling down of the stronghold of evil and an invaluable asset for the building up of the body of Christ.

11

The Minister and His Gift

It is a mischievous fallacy which haunts many people that the supernatural gifts of the Holy Spirit operate spontaneously; so that, so long as the possessor does not willfully "quench the Spirit," he has very little responsibility in the matter.

No doubt this idea has gained ground because the conception which many people have of "spiritual gifts" is limited to the gifts of inspired utterance—prophecy, tongues, and interpretation.

Yet even in these gifts the possessor carries a large share of personal responsibility. "The spirits of the prophets are subject to the prophets" (1 Corinthians

14:32), and it is the responsibility of the believer to see that such a gift is only exercised on fitting occasions (v. 28), in proper order (v. 27), and with due self-control (v. 30). The inspiration of the Holy Spirit operating in conformity with the law of divine love (chapter 13) is far removed from the frenzied outbursts of those "carried away" (12:2) by demon power. There is spontaneity, but its spring is in divine order.

The Gift for Ministry—Revealed

The responsibility of the believer begins as soon as he knows—either by a divine revelation, or by a discovery of it in exercise—that the Lord has granted him some gift. "The manifestation of the Spirit is given to every man *to profit withal*" (1 Corinthians 12:7). The principle is contained in the parable of the talents. The Master's goods are to be traded with: the faithful servant must "occupy till I come."

A frequent question is, "How shall I *know* that I have some ministry gift from Christ?" The answer is that you will know in the same way that you know you have certain natural gifts. The parent will carefully watch the child finishing its education, to discover what natural bent it displays that may indicate future career —either mechanical, artistic, commercial, scholastic, or whatnot. So in the spiritual, the Spirit-gifted child of God called to fill some definite office of ministry in the church will quickly display well-marked capabilities along a certain line. These will be further proved as coming from the Lord by the fact that blessing will quickly begin to result, the "talent" will begin to make other talents (as in the case of Philip's first evangelistic ministry in Samaria, Acts 8). Moreover, the church as a body will have a clear witness that such a one has a definite ministry entrusted to him from the Lord. (Note how the apostles surnamed Barnabas, "the son of consolation" or "exhortation" rather. Acts 4:36.)

If the gift given to the believer is revealed by a prophetic utterance (as in the case of 1 Timothy 4:14), then we may be sure its presence will quickly be proved in actual exercise—unless the possessor is hopelessly unfaithful.

Every believer who has been filled with the Holy Spirit should examine himself with a view to understanding what particular ministry he has received from the Lord.

The Gift for Ministry—Exercised

As soon as a child of God realizes that the Lord has placed within him a power for service, he should pray very earnestly that the divine purpose might be completely fulfilled with regard to it; and at the same time he should diligently seek to understand all he can regarding the divine method of working in these things.

Here comes in the danger, already noted, of thinking that spiritual gifts operate automatically. Paul's urge to Timothy is sufficient to correct this error, for he makes it a matter for the young man's own responsibility to "neglect not the gift," but to "stir up the gift that is in thee" (2 Timothy 1:6). This is considerably removed from that dreamy "waiting for the moving of the waters" attitude which some Spirit-filled believers have mistakenly adopted regarding the exercise of their gift and ministry.

The responsibility of the minister to his gift is threefold, as revealed in Romans 12:6-8:

(a) *Faith must be kept strong* (v. 6). "Prophesy according to the proportion of faith" (v. 6). This particularly applies to gifts and ministries of inspired utterance —to "prophets." Unless their vision and spiritual grasp of the unseen and eternal remains strong and virile their particular line of ministry will quickly lose its power.

Of course this principle applies with equal force all round. Waning faith will sap the absolute lifeblood out of any one of the ministry gifts of Christ. The minister who wants to maintain his gift at the zenith of blessing must carefully nourish his own faith by times of communion with God, and by feeding his soul on the Word of God. Not less must he sanctify himself from all that knowingly weakens and drags him in vision down to the level of the natural man, whether it be books, friends, occupations, or things otherwise legitimate. He is a spiritual athlete, and must keep himself in rigid training. His *faith* is vital.

(b) *We must "wait" upon our Ministry* (v. 7). This particularly applies to pastors and teachers, but it is likewise a principle for all. Time *must* be diligently given to the perfecting and maintaining of our God-given ministry at its proper standard of usefulness—and of all things in "Pentecostal" ministry, this seems the least understood. For a teacher to spend time in study and preparation, and to seek to perfect the divine gift within him by systematic training and every legitimate means in his power, is often regarded as "carnal"! It is high time that we clearly understood from the Scriptures as well as from experience that the gift of Christ imparts *power* for the ministry, but the fulfillment of that ministry rests upon the faithful use by the minister of his gift.

Moreover, when a man realizes that he has received a certain ministry from the Lord upon a well-defined line, then he should particularly "wait" upon his own gift so that he becomes expert in it and can "excel to the edifying of the church" (1 Corinthians 14:12); rather than allow himself to be distracted with a whole multitude of offices which are no integral part of his own call from

God (Acts 6:2). Such a man will never make the most of his own proper gift.

(c) *We need qualities of character* (v. 8). "With simplicity," "with diligence," "with cheerfulness," is the threefold reminder that it is not only what we do, but how we do it, that makes our exercise of ministry gifts well-pleasing to God and a blessing to men.

The personal character of the minister always brings in a vital element with regard to the fruit which will accrue from his ministry. Even spiritual gifts, "however excellent, are nothing worth without charity," as Paul plainly shows in 1 Corinthians 13. A keeper of the vineyards must diligently keep the vineyard of his own soul, not only for the sake of his own personal reward, but for the sheer necessity of maintaining his gift from the Lord in blessing.

How often a glorious gift from God is spoiled by hardness or pride or greed in the one who exercises it. Such inconsistency not only grieves the church, but it absolutely repels the world. And sooner or later it is bound to come out, however much the brilliance of the gift may temporarily blind the eyes of the multitude. This ultimately makes a ministry gift useless, and worse than useless, for it drags the very name of the Giver into reproach and shame. Inspiration does not sanctify; but how deeply inspiration needs sanctification if it is going to fulfill the will of God.

The Gift for Ministry—Buried

This is a possibility not so remote as many imagine. The fact that in His parable of the talents (Matthew 25) our Lord devotes so much time to the principle illustrated by the unprofitable servant who "digged in the earth and hid his lord's money" (not his own money, be it noted) implies that Christ's disciples *need* such strong teaching. It is not a question of *losing* the gift, or of the gift being taken away (until after the "reckoning"). The gift remains intact in the possession of the servant, and is delivered up intact when he meets the Lord (v. 25). The whole point is that the possessor *did nothing with it*. Paul evidently feared that Timothy might make this very failure, and in a lesser degree some of the Roman Christians also.

The possession of a ministry gift from Christ involves a great personal responsibility—a responsibility measured only by the exeeding gravity of our Lord's words concerning the servant who took no steps to insure his talents "gaining" something.

It is a solemn thing to remember that a gift which I may not have been exercising, or an office which I may not have been filling for years, is still with me and must inevitably be accounted for.

In this connection not only individuals but whole assemblies and whole movements need to watch lest spiritual gifts which they still believe in *on paper* have ceased to be operative in their midst. For all practical purposes they have "hidden" their Lord's money and have certainly taken away all possibility of its making any increase. There is no virtue in believing in the ministry gifts of Christ theoretically unless we are striving to have them in continual and fruitful exercise. But this is sometimes a costly business! It is easier to dig and hide and mistakenly comfort our consciences with the thought that we have not really *lost* our gift, but shall be able to return it to the Lord intact when He returns. But what about His parable?

Still one other phase of this vital question of our responsibility is taught by Paul in 1 Corinthians 13 and 14, when he points out that even in the exercise of gifts we have to see that they are really building up something of eternal value (14:12, 26). There can be an exercise of gifts which is gaining practically nothing (13:1-3; 14:6; 14:23). He sums up his own tremendous earnestness in this matter when he says, "I had rather speak five words with my understanding, that by my voice I might teach others also, than ten thousand words in an unknown tongue" (v. 17). This does *not* mean, as so many would hastily infer, that Paul has no use for the gift of tongues; the context proves very differently from that. But it *does* mean that the constraining determination of every possessor of any spiritual gift should be that his gift is yielding something of genuine profit among men, for the glory of the Giver.

12

The Ministry Gifts in the Lord Jesus

One of the most delightful aspects of the subject we have been considering is to be found in tracing each one of the great ministry gifts in the person and work of the Lord Jesus Christ.

We are distinctly told that Christ is the Head . . . "from whom all the body fitly joined together and compacted by that which every joint supplieth . . . maketh increase" (Ephesians 4:15,16). It is therefore to be expected that those ministries which we possess as different members of that body (1 Corinthians 12) will all find manifestation and supreme expression in the Lord as our Head. And this we find to be literally true and capable of Scriptural demonstration.

Christ—the Apostle

"Consider the Apostle . . . of our profession, Christ Jesus" (Hebrews 3:1). How perfectly He fulfills the qualifications which that great office demands.

In the first place He was the "Sent One" from God— the One "whom the Father hath sanctified, and *sent* into the world" (John 10:36; 17:18). He said of Himself, "I came down from heaven not to do mine own will, but the will of him that *sent* me." (John 6:38). Obedience to every step of the predetermined pathway the Father had "sent" Him to fulfill (Acts 2:23; 4:28) was the keynote of His life, death, and resurrection. The Lord who sent His apostles forth with their great commission was first of all fully obedient to His own great commission.

He was an Apostle also in the sense of being a pioneer in the truest sense. He is the "Author" of our faith (Hebrews 12:2). He came to do even more than preach the gospel—He came to *make* a gospel of the grace of God by His atoning sacrifice that *could* be preached wherever man is found. And for this He had to "tread the winepress alone." Glorious pioneer of our redemption!

Moreover, He was, and is, the great Church Builder. Note carefully His own words in Matthew 16:18 (for they are often misinterpreted): "Upon this rock will *I* build my church." It was not Peter, or any of the apostles, however faithfully they might discharge their office, who were in the final analysis to be the real planters and establishers of churches. The apostle may establish local assemblies, but the builder of that Church which is the whole body is none less than the great Apostle of our faith; and unless we have been built in by Him "as living stones" (1 Peter 2:5) our hope is in vain.

Christ—the Prophet

That Christ was a "prophet mighty in deed and word before God and all the people" (Luke 24:19) is a fact testified to in the Scriptures continually (Matthew (21:11; Luke 7:16; John 9:17). More than that, He was essentially *the Prophet* whose coming was foretold by Moses (Deuteronomy 18:18; John 6:14; 7:40; Acts 3:22).

The Holy Spirit rested upon Him in a continual anointing, so that His words always came forth as inspired revelation of the very heart and mind of God (John 3:34; 6:68; 14:24).

Moreover, the searching nature of such inspired ministry, which is stated by Paul in 1 Corinthians 14:25 concerning the effect of prophetic ministry in the Church—"Thus are the secrets of his heart made manifest"—was strikingly manifested in our Lord. The woman of Samaria said with startled emphasis after His words had probed her heart, "Sir, I perceive that thou art a *prophet*" (John 4:19). She was only one of many others who felt the same power.

The prophet is also preeminently the one who reveals the emotion of God to the people; and Christ did this of a truth. His revelation of the heart of the Father in tender emotion contained in the parable of the prodigal son in superb (Luke 15:20). One of the most intensely emotional passages in literature, combining also pure prediction, is to be found in His sobbing declaration over the Holy City, immediately following His own claim that He was a prophet—"O Jerusalem, Jerusalem, which killest the prophets, . . . your house is left unto you desolate. . . . Ye shall not see me, until the time come when ye shall say, Blessed is He that cometh in the name of the Lord" (Luke 13:33-35). Truly He was a "Prophet."

Christ—the Evangelist

From the very outset of His public ministry, Christ was a Preacher of the good news of redeeming love to the people. He stands in the synagogue at Nazareth and says the Lord "hath anointed me to preach the gospel to the poor; he hath sent me to heal the brokenhearted; to preach deliverance to the captives; and recovering of sight to the blind; to set at liberty them that are bruised; to preach the acceptable year of the Lord" (Luke 4:18,19). There probably cannot be found anywhere a more perfect epitome of a true evangelist's ministry.

Moreover, He combined the healing of the sick with the preaching of the Word (Matthew 4:23; 9:35), and thus gave the personal precedent for those whom He afterwards sent forth to evangelize, and combine in their evangelism the same twin ministries (Matthew, 10:7, 8; Acts 8:5-8; 14:7-10). It is specially beautiful and suggestive to note that the spring of this fragrant evangelism of our Lord's was *compassion* for the multitude (Matthew 9:36; 14:14). This is ever the spring of true evangelism.

We should do well also to note that this divine compassion of the Master's did not expend itself in only preaching the gospel to the hungry multitudes. He saw them "scattered abroad, as sheep having no shepherd." Souls of men need more than evangelizing; they need shepherding; so this leads us to see

Christ—the Pastor

There is wonderful revelation of Christ as the ideal Pastor when we remember that the words "pastor" and "shepherd" are both translations of the same Greek word, *poimen.* He was the "Good Shepherd" who gave His life for the sheep (John 10:11); He is the "Great

Shepherd" of the whole flock of God, who has been brought again from the dead (Hebrews 13:20); and we shall some day see Him as the "Chief Shepherd," when He shall appear to give to His faithful servants a crown of glory (1 Peter 5:4). How exquisite also is the revelation of His tenderness as a shepherd gathering "the lambs with his arm" (Isaiah 40:11).

Christ is the supreme Pastor of "all the flock . . . which he hath purchased with his own blood" (Acts 20:28). When human pastors fail or when the comfort of earthly ministries is denied us, then every believer can appropriate the direct pastoral care of the Lord Himself, and say triumphantly with David "The *Lord* is my shepherd; I shall not want" (Psalms 23:1).

And there is comfort also for the pastors themselves, often the loneliest of men spiritually by virtue of their office, in the fact that they also have a "Pastor," a "Chief Shepherd," who knows all about the burdens of the pastoral office and the "care of all the churches," for He understands. Thank God the pastors have a *pastor*.

Christ—the Teacher

The whole world today unites in chorus with the testimony of Nicodemus concerning Christ—"We know that thou art a teacher come from God" (John 3:2). As a Teacher He stands supreme.

What lessons those who seek to teach in His name can learn at His feet: His simplicity of style and utterances, so that children can understand His meaning; His clarity of thought, so that moral issues are never blurred or indistinct (it is always heaven or hell, life or death, light or darkness, salvation or destruction with Him); His charming method of illustration from the most familiar things of daily life in the home, the farm, or the market. Yet with it all there was the everpresent note of authority (Matthew 7:29). The trumpet gave no uncertain note for the battle.

His ministry of teaching was also just as much from a spring of compassion for the multitude as was His evangelism (Mark 6:34). No pride, no mere love of displaying superior knowledge, but a pure longing to help men in their perplexity and hunger after truth.

And then He left them, after His expositions of the Scripture, with hearts that burned (Luke 24:32). There was none of the letter that killeth, but always the spirit that giveth life.

Paul writes a very striking thing in this fourth chapter to the Ephesians which we have been studying so much. In verses 20 and 21 he says, "But ye have not so learned Christ; if so be that ye have *heard him,* and have been *taught by him,* as the truth is in Jesus."

What did Paul mean? Christ had never visited Ephesus. These Gentile believers had never heard the voice that preached in Galilee. And yet they had. Paul declares it, and our own hearts and our own experience confirm the truth of his words, and we understand what he meant.

In every one of the genuine ministry gifts of Christ there comes again, through the members of the Body the voice of the Head. In a true apostle there is the Spirit of Christ, the Great Apostle of our profession, planting, building, and leading onward; in a true prophet there is speaking once again the voice that Christ's own sheep always recognize; in every true evangelist the Spirit of Christ is again seeking with tender compassion the lost sheep over the mountains; in the sacrificial ministry of each true pastor the Good Shepherd is again giving His life for the sheep; while through every teacher given by Him, the Spirit of truth is taking the things of Christ and revealing them unto us.

In the ministry gifts of Christ, He who ever liveth ministers continually from the throne. And that is perhaps the greatest thing of all that we can say about the ministry gifts.